1st
10-19

MARRIAGE MAKEOVER

MARRIAGE MAKEOVER

SIMPLE WAYS TO REVITALIZE YOUR RELATIONSHIP . . . WITHOUT YOUR SPOUSE EVEN KNOWING

BARBARA BARTLEIN

TURNER

Turner Publishing Company

200 4th Avenue North • Suite 950
Nashville, Tennessee 37219

445 Park Avenue • 9th Floor
New York, NY 10022

www.turnerpublishing.com

Marriage Makeover:
Simple Ways to Revitalize Your Relationship . . . Without Your Spouse Even Knowing

Cover design by Mike Penticost
Art direction by Gina Binkley
Cover image courtesy of Bridgeman Art Library

Library of Congress Cataloging-in-Publication Data

Bartlein, Barbara, 1951-
 Marriage makeover : simple ways to revitalize your relationship--without your
spouse even knowing / Barbara Bartlein.
    p. cm.
 Rev. ed. of: 75 things to improve your marriage without your spouse knowing
it.
 Includes bibliographical references.
 ISBN 978-1-59652-829-1
 1. Marriage. 2. Married people--Psychology. 3. Man-woman relationships.
 I. Bartlein, Barbara, 1951- 75 things to improve your marriage without your
spouse knowing it. II. Title.
 HQ734.B2747 2011
 646.7'8--dc23

2011018431

Printed in the United States of America
11 12 13 14 15 16 17—0 9 8 7 6 5 4 3 2 1

This book is also available in gift book format as
75 Things To Improve Your Marriage Without Your Spouse Even Knowing
(978-1-59652-750-8)

To Charlie

Contents

Acknowledgements

I wish to sincerely thank all the wonderful people who have encouraged and supported me through the writing of this book. This includes Michael McCalip and Todd Bottorff at Turner Publishing for their ideas. My editor and son, Ken Brosky, from Final Draft Literary, who advised me on content and structure.

A special thank you to the Between the Lines Book Club, who offered their expertise on men, women, and relationships. This includes Maggie Smith, Mary Vitrano, Shari Kaplan Paler, Cindy Barnicki, Judy Perkins, Mary Fitzpatrick, Jane Wood, Deb Markoff, and Francine Gill. I could not have written this book without your hilarious input.

I appreciate all the encouragement and support from my mother, Wilma Gunther. I have been so blessed to have you all these years. Thank you to my daughter, Stephanie, who tells me "just get to work," and my niece Jocelyn, who makes every day full of sunshine. A special appreciation to Dagny Holt and Roger Marquass for joining in the fun at our house. We love you both.

And hugs and kisses to my husband of more than thirty years, Charlie. You seem to get better with age and will always be my best friend.

How is the health of your relationship?

The best relationships are friendships that catch fire. How well do you know your partner and their view of the world? Answer the following questions to find out.

1. I understand my partner's philosophies about life.   Yes No

2. I consider my partner to be my very best friend.   Yes No

3. We often touch and kiss for no particular reason.   Yes No

4. I call my partner several times a day.   Yes No

5. I understand my partner's dreams for the future.   Yes No

6. We find our sex life is fun and satisfying.   Yes No

7. We touch base every day about how our day is going.   Yes No

8. If I have a problem, I talk with my partner.   Yes No

9. We have scheduled activities that we look forward to.   Yes No

10. We have similar values and goals.   Yes No

11. I think my partner has high integrity.   Yes No

12. I can't wait to get home at the end of the day.   Yes No

13. We have favorite traditions for many of the holidays.   Yes No

14. I feel that my partner respects me.   Yes No

15. We enjoy many of the same activities.   Yes No

16. My partner understands my family.   Yes No

17. My partner makes me laugh.   Yes No

How many "Yes" answers did you have?

15 or more: You have a strong relationship built on
                   friendship.

9-14:   You have a good base but additional
                   work will enhance your relationship.
                   This is a good time to utilize the sugges-
                   tions and ideas in this book.

8 or fewer: Get busy or you and your partner risk
                   drifting apart.

Introduction

Couples often wonder how they can improve their marriages and may invest considerable time, money, and effort in classes, counseling, and "encounter" weekends to find the answers. More often, though, they do nothing. They settle into a daily routine that is busy and demanding with little time to think about, let alone implement, improvements to their marriage.

Marriages cannot move forward on autopilot. I have seen more marriages go out with a whimper than an explosion. Couples report, "We simply grew apart," or "We no longer enjoy the same things," or "We just didn't have time for each other." They drift through their busy lives, putting the marriage on the back burner. They are then surprised when the fire fizzles out.

While 70 percent of adult Americans believe that marriage is a lifelong commitment, the statistics for marriage are dismal. First marriages have a 45 percent chance of breaking up, and second marriages have a 60 percent chance of divorce.[1] "Divorced person" is currently the fastest-growing marital status category, with the number of divorced adults quadrupling from 4.3 million in 1970 to 17.4 million in 1994.[2]

Your marriage, however, does not need to succumb to these statistics. With just a little effort you can create everyday experiences that weave together to strengthen, enhance, and grow your marriage. And there are good reasons to do so.

According to research, married people are the happiest. They report less depression, less anxiety, and lower levels of other types of psychological distress than do those who are single, divorced, or widowed. In fact, marital status is one of the most important predictors of happiness, with 40 percent of married folks saying they are very happy with their life in general, as compared with just under 25 percent of those who are single or who are cohabiting.[3]

Marrieds are also healthier and live longer than their single counterparts. Unmarrieds have significantly higher rates of mortality: 50 percent higher among women and 250 percent higher among men. The unmarried are far more likely to die from all causes, including coronary heart disease, stroke, pneumonia, cancer, cirrhosis, automobile accidents, murder, and suicide. Researchers have found that there are even positive effects from the "nag factor"—the routine nagging that spouses engage in actually encourages a positive lifestyle and decreases destructive habits such as smoking or drinking to excess.

A healthy marriage may also be the starting point for a growing net worth. Not only is divorce very costly in the short run, but the long-term effects of not being married dramatically affect how financially secure you become. The longer people stay married, the greater the wealth they accumulate. At retirement, a typical married couple has accumulated about $410,000, compared with about $167,000 for the never-married, about $145,000 for the divorced, and just under $96,000 for the separated. This could be owing in part to the fact that married people behave more responsibly when it comes to money because they have more responsibilities. By pooling money, labor, and time, married people create far more opportunities for building wealth.[4]

Spouses also have better access to health and life insurance coverage, pensions, and Social Security. Being married also provides its own additional "insurance," since spouses almost always leave their worldly goods and benefits to their partners.

There is even a value to in-laws. They tend to help a family when needed. In-laws also provide potential access to inheritance. In the past five years, about 29 percent of married couples received financial help from in-laws, and about 25 percent of families with children received financial transfers.[5]

Out of all the reasons to work on your marriage, one of the most important is that it is fun. There is a lot of happiness in spending years with someone and building a secure and satisfying life. Implement just a few of these ideas and you will see your relationship blossom.

Part I: Doing favors

Happy couples practice the art of kindness in everyday life by doing favors for their spouses. These small gestures make your partner's life just a little bit easier or simpler. They provide a lift on a stressful day or joy on a sunny one. Your special treatment sends a powerful message that you care, are thinking of them, and are paying attention.

Research on married couples has shown that you need six positive interactions for every negative encounter.[6] Without positive interaction, it can feel like the two of you are always butting heads. Favors give you an opportunity to increase the connection with your spouse. They build good will and friendship.

Tom Wolfe, in his novel *Bonfire of the Vanities,* talks about the "favor bank" system, in which Irish cops, judges, and lawyers do favors for one another with the understanding that when they need a favor their "friends" will come through for them. Everyone has a full bank account of favors. A full bank account of favors means that your spouse has done so many helpful and kind things for you that you are more than willing to reciprocate.

These favors are not viewed as a burden or chore. Rather, they are an opportunity to express your love and caring in another way. Often, the process is even more enjoyable for you than it is for your spouse. Here are some ideas to pamper your partner.

Fill up the gas tank

There is a great *Seinfeld* episode where Kramer and a car sales-man decide to take a test ride in a new vehicle. They drive several miles on the freeway and then decide that they want to see how far they can go on a tank of gas. Imitating a scene from *Thelma and Louise,* they refuse to stop until they are driving on fumes, missing exit after exit with great excitement.

For many of us, this is reality; we try to see how far we can go on a tank of gas. We dread the inevitable chore of filling up the tank. We procrastinate, hoping the price will go down. Or we avoid the pumps because we are short on time or money. Then that annoying little light, in the shape of a gas pump, illuminates, warning of impending doom if we do not immediately pull over and swipe our card for the petrol.

This is precisely why a full tank of gas is such a nice surprise. To get in your car, glance at the gauge, and see the tank past the full mark is true joy. You know immediately, of course, who filled the tank. Certainly, no neighbor siphoned the liquid energy in for you. No, it must have been your sweet lover.

Not only have you been saved from having to deal with the hassle of pumping your gas, you can sit secure knowing that you have at least a week or two before you have to think about it again. And if you had two twenties in your wallet to purchase gas, then all the better.

This is a favor that can be done anytime you see that your spouse's fuel gauge is low. Of course, you can add the frosting on the cake to this favor by washing the windshield or even the entire car. When my husband really wants to impress, he vacuums the inside and throws away the junk.

Change their watch battery

I have had a wonderful Gucci watch for years. It has bands of different colors that can be screwed around the face of the watch to match whatever outfit I might be wearing. There is even a diamond band that can be used when I want to dress it up. I love it, except when it's time to find a battery.

I have gone back to the store where I bought it only to be told they no longer carry the watch or the batteries. I have gone to jewelers, kiosks at the mall, and specialty shops. Everyone says the same thing: "Great watch! But a real pain to put a battery in. We don't work on them anymore." But I still love the watch.

You can imagine my excitement when my husband informed me that he had found a place to buy the watch battery. And, he had a new one put in without my even asking. I was back in business with my favorite watch. He definitely got points on that one.

Watch batteries are just one of those little hassles in life, even if your watch situation isn't as challenging as mine. Your spouse will appreciate it if you make an extra stop and take care of this.

Put their favorite magazine in the bathroom

A friend of mine has a husband who travels extensively for his job. She can't always wait up for him because he returns home late at night, exhausted and road burned. But she makes sure he is welcomed home by putting the latest sports page in the bathroom for his evening reading. Nice touch. She lets him know that she has been thinking of him with this little extra effort.

A lot of people like to read in the bathroom. Some even find it necessary to satisfactorily accomplish the task at hand. For many men, it is almost a zen-like experience. A room that my husband affectionately refers to as "the library," the bathroom is a place of leisure and relaxation.

A little attention to the reading material in this private room can pay big dividends. *Newsweek,* the *Wall Street Journal,* and the *National Review* are great publications for this purpose. You can also get specialty books, like the *Uncle John's Bathroom Reading* series, which has short, quick articles that are fun and interesting.

I have the *Uncle John's All Purpose Extra Strength Bathroom*

Reader on hand in my powder room. It has everything from the origins of the telephone booth to animals famous for fifteen minutes. I get completely engrossed in the description of Mary Wollstonecraft and her novel *Frankenstein,* and then review the *Wide World of Weird Sports,* which includes toe wrestling and grenade throwing. Each chapter is a quick read with interesting facts and ideas.

The bathroom, also known as the thinking room, is where critical decisions are made. According to AskMen.com, here are the top ten things that are great to read in the bathroom:

1. *Archie Comics.* Or any comics for that matter. They are simple, straightforward, and escapist literature for the not-too-serious sessions.
2. *Leonard Maltin's Movie & Video Guide.* Picking movies to rent and TIVO can be a daunting task, so here is the answer. Accomplish two tasks at the same time: your daily visit and your evening rental.
3. *TV Guide.* Just take a highlighter in there with you and plan your entire TV schedule in one sitting. If you have a busy week scheduled, you can circle the shows to tape.
4. *Chicken Soup for the Soul.* There are hundreds to choose from but they all follow the same format: lots of short stories about overcoming life's obstacles and challenges. Check out the ones with stories from yours truly: "Chicken Soup for the Nurse's Soul," "Christmas Cheer," and "Chicken Soup for the Caregiver's Soul."
5. *The daily newspaper.* If you are still receiving a paper copy, it's nice to just throw it in the bathroom for later. At least you will have time to check out the day's headlines.
6. *The Ultimate Bathroom Reader.* The title says it all. It is chock-full of interesting tidbits that you can quote at the next party and impress your friends.

7. *Business magazines.* Good chance to catch up with the latest trends and career advice. Most issues are divided into short articles, so they work well for this purpose.
8. *A dictionary or encyclopedia.* Why not get a little smarter each day? You'll be amazed how quickly you can learn new words and information.
9. *Playboy or Playgirl.* For those so disposed. And don't use the "I like the articles" excuse.
10. *Guinness Book of World Records.* Don't knock this until you've tried it. It is fascinating reading and will give you all sorts of useless information.

Whatever the interests at your house, surprise your partner with a favorite magazine or newspaper. It will be appreciated.

Offer to bring them something

I know this dates me, but I remember TV before we had remote controls. Actually, I even remember TV when it went off the air, and all we got to see was the test pattern. But the point is, before remote controls, you had to rise out of your chair and walk across the room to change a channel or turn up the volume. For some TV bugs, this was as close to an exercise program as they ever experienced.

This all changed in the 1950s when Zenith invented the first TV remote control, appropriately called "Lazy Bones." Remotes became the rage, and a "must have" for any TV owner. They made it easy for us to plant ourselves in overstuffed furniture for a good part of the day without moving—a state of being referred to as "couch potato."

This is precisely why it is so nice to offer to get your spouse something if you get up. After all, you are up. Your spouse is down. If you have had a long, strenuous day, it's nice to be down. There has to be a good reason to get up. Now that you are up, you may as well maximize the effort to see what else you can accomplish. It's a nice gesture to offer to get something for someone else.

Offers like, "Can I freshen your drink?" "Would you like a pretzel?" "Can I get you something?" are easy to fulfill and will be much appreciated.

You can extend this idea and offer at other times as well, of course. Is your partner not feeling well? Ask him if he would like something from the pharmacy. Is she falling asleep on the couch? Get her a comfy pillow from the bed. She complains of feeling cold? Grab the blanket off the couch and help her snuggle in. These little things mean a lot and let your spouse know that you really care.

Remember their parents' birthdays

I'm sure there are guys out there who remember birthdays and send hand-picked, thoughtful cards. I just haven't met any. Seriously, in reviewing most of the couples and friends I know, the woman is in charge here. If it were left to the guys, no one would ever get a card.

This is precisely why it is so helpful if you, as the wife, remember the in-laws on their special day. Yes, your husband will get the credit, but secretly your mother-in-law knows only too well who sent it, because she never received a card before you came into the picture.

It is said that women are the "emotional managers" in a family. I think that is true. We tend to be the ones who remember events, make doctor appointments, and manage the Christmas card list. But you can make the process of card sending a lot easier by devising a system.

I use Microsoft Outlook for my birthday and anniversary reminders. You simply put into the program all the events that you want to celebrate, and it creates a "reminder" that will alert you when you specify. I set it for three days' advance notice, so that I have plenty of time to get the card, sign it, and put it in the mail.

To make things even easier, I usually buy cards for the whole year. That way, I am not running out at the last minute to get just one card. I find that airports are great places to find creative cards, and I often stock up while waiting for a flight. If you really want to simplify the whole process, you can use Web sites like Hallmark. com to have the cards sent automatically.

Leave the light on if they are late

Leaving a light on is as American as mothers and apple pie. Like a beacon in a storm, it provides a guide to home and family. In other words, it helps you to feel welcomed. Like many people, I hate coming home to a completely dark house with everyone in bed. It feels like the store closed without you.

Leave a light on when your spouse is still out. If you know he or she hasn't eaten dinner, it is also great if you put a plate of food in the refrigerator. "Real food" is so much nicer than a bag of stale potato chips. And if you really want to score some points, leave a little love note that lets him know you are waiting for him.

Some folks do more elaborate things, like a series of notes directing the latecomer where to go, or a trail of rose petals leading to the bedroom. This is a little too dramatic for me. I simply leave the porch and kitchen lights on. He knows where to find me.

Get an oil change for the car

Automobiles are a drain of time, money, and energy. This is why any assistance with this metal sieve is always appreciated. True, some folks are thrilled with a new car, spending $20,000, $40,000, and even more for a hunk of metal that depreciates the minute they drive it off the lot. Surround sound, heated seats, built-in GPS systems, and OnStar have turned our vehicles into second homes. Personally, I hate what they cost and wish I could just walk or bike everywhere.

But cars are a necessity and since they cost so much, it's wise to take care of them. At our house, we drive our cars right into the ground, literally pushing them into the junkyard as they heave their last sigh. We consider ourselves to have failed if we get less than 250,000 miles on a vehicle. The secret to this longevity is in great measure the oil change.

We are almost religious about getting oil changes every 3,500 miles, and we put a lot of miles on our cars. That means that one of our cars needs a change every couple of weeks. No matter how "instant" the oil change is supposed to be, you still have to drive, wait, and sit there to make it happen.

It comes as a real relief when someone does this for you. When my husband offers to do this chore, I pack him up with a Starbucks coffee and today's newspaper and send him out the door. Excellent. He has just saved me at least two hours of time. And when I see the new sticker on the windshield, I know I don't have to deal with this hassle for a while.

Light the fireplace

There is something special about sitting in front of a fire. It feels so romantic, warm, and calming. We are fortunate to have two fireplaces in our home. Yet, for years we rarely used them. It was just too much of a hassle to start the fire with some newspaper, find kindling, add the logs, and get the darn thing going. Once it was blazing, the fire still needed tending, logs needed adding, and we had to make sure sparks didn't fly out to singe the carpet.

Once the fire was burning, someone also had to make sure that it went out. No problem if we were going to hang out all night, but definitely an issue if we wanted to leave or go to bed early. And then when it was all over, we had to clean up the mess. Sigh.

Several years ago, we decided we wanted more fires with a lot less hassle. We converted one fireplace to gas. We don't get the wood smell or the crackling of a wood fire, but we sure have a lot more fires. Now we use the fireplace all the time. I love to light it before my husband comes home to heat up the family room. He likes to light it when we are watching a good movie and all the other lights are out. Sometimes we light it and just snuggle on the couch.

If you are like us and find that a wood-burning fireplace is just too much trouble, convert to gas and light it up. If you don't have one, consider putting one in.

Let them know what you want for special occasions

Do everyone a favor and don't play the "glass head" game. You know what I mean: expecting your spouse to simply read your mind and know what you want for your birthday, Christmas, or anniversary. I hear this all the time: "If he really loves me, he will know what I want," "If she really cared, she would know how I feel."

Let's just all admit it—we don't know. Isn't life complicated enough without this game involved in every event and every holiday? Let's just all tell each other what we really want. Your spouse will be relieved and you dramatically increase the chances that you will get what you really want.

I learned this lesson a long time ago when my husband gave me vacuum cleaner bags for our first anniversary. He thought it was funny, exclaiming, "Well, the first year is paper." I wasn't laughing.

He then said words to me I have never forgotten. "You know, most of the time I don't even know what I'm thinking. I certainly don't know what you're thinking. If you really want something, just ask." I have been asking ever since.

I pick out jewelry, new golf clubs, and vacation weekends. I suggest good restaurants and concerts. Yes, I know that some of you will say that this is not romantic. "If they really cared, they would just know." Well, if that is working for you, fine. Me? I got vacuum cleaner bags.

Change the lightbulbs

Burned-out lightbulbs are so annoying, especially when you flip the switch and they burn out instantly with a big flash. Almost as if we are in complete denial, we tend to flip the switch on and off several times to learn whether the bulb really burned out. It did. Of course, we forget all about changing the bulb until we flip that switch again in a couple of days and realize we're still in the dark.

Keep a ready supply of various watts of lightbulbs, and change the bulbs as soon as they burn out. Don't wait until someone trips in the dark or falls down the stairs. And don't wait until your spouse points it out.

Hand them a warm towel
after a shower

Few things are more wonderful than getting out of the tub or shower and wrapping up, taco style, in a warm towel. Especially on a cold winter day, this extra warmth feels delicious and decadent. For some of us, it takes us back to our childhoods when Mom brought towels fresh out of the dryer for the after-bath rubdown.

The Europeans have the right idea. At even modest hotels throughout Europe, bathrooms come equipped with electric towel warmers. Of various designs and finishes, they hang on the wall or sit on the floor and produce radiant heat through their grills.

Towel warmers not only ensure that the towels are warm and dry each time you use them, they also warm the area of the shower or bath they occupy. I got hooked on them the first time I traveled to Europe. (Unlike the bidets, which still seem ridiculous to me.)

You can buy towel warmers for your own house, relatively inexpensively. One site to check out is www.signaturehardware.

com. They sell a number of different electric towel warmers, some for under $100.

They are well worth the money, and they don't use much electricity. But there are other ways to get the same effect. You can put towels in the oven for a few minutes or in the dryer on high. If you have a fireplace, warm them up beside the fire. Some people microwave their towels, but I don't think this works as well. The easiest way is to just offer a warm towel fresh out of the dryer when you are doing the laundry anyway.

Does this sound like too much trouble? That is exactly why it's so effective. Of course it's a hassle. That's the point. We can get so caught up in the things we have to do that we forget to enjoy the things we want to do. It will be appreciated by your spouse because it makes the moment so special.

Put some extra money in their pocket (or purse)

Like many married couples, we really don't have "my" money and "your" money. Our finances are lumped together in one checking account. But there is something about cash that makes me feel rich, especially if I don't expect it.

This is the only reason that I like doing the laundry. There are usually a few stray bills that come out of the dryer, and the rule is they are mine. I quickly stuff them into my pocket like a just reward for a dirty job.

I love finding a little extra cash in a pocket or purse, as well. It's like money falling out of the sky. It gives me a good excuse to treat myself at Starbucks or buy a lunch out. I have no qualms about spending it, because I wasn't expecting it in the first place.

People love finding money they were unaware that they already had. There is a page on Facebook.com called "Finding Money In Your Pocket," with a picture of $20 bills in a jeans pocket. Last I checked, the page had 3,490,097 visitors who had clicked the "Like" button.

Add to these numbers by surprising your partner. Stick ten bucks in his jacket or into the cup holder in her car.

Do something you don't want to do

Married couples don't need to do everything together, but it sure is nice to have some things you both enjoy. These common interests give you things to talk and laugh about. You can plan ahead and have events to look forward to. But what if your spouse really likes something that you can't stand? Well, maybe you should do it anyway.

When I say do it anyway, I mean without complaining, whining, and sulking. Don't keep a running commentary of why you aren't having a good time, how bad the event is, and pointing out that the seats are uncomfortable. Refrain from commenting on the sound, temperature, and other attendees at the event. Just sit there and assure your spouse you are having a good time.

Why, you ask? Because sometimes in a marriage you just do things that you really don't want to do. You do them because you care about your spouse and it's important to her. You do it so that maybe, on occasion, she will also reciprocate. And you just might even find something new to enjoy.

I never was much of a football fan, but I married a man who is addicted to the Green Bay Packers. He has stuck with them through thick and thin and never misses a game. Me? It always struck me as a waste of time on a Sunday afternoon.

Then I went to Lambeau Field for a home game. Located in the heart of Green Bay, it's a historic stadium that doesn't have a bad seat. Opened in 1957, and renovated a number of times, it now holds 72,928 screaming, wild Packers fans. And these fans are unique creatures. They paint their bodies green and gold, wear cheese heads, and cheer on the team in weather 30 degrees below zero. I always thought it was crazy. But then I experienced it for myself. After watching Brett Favre in action, I was hooked. Now, I never miss a game.

I have Packers shirts, Packers hats, and Packers displays on the front porch. I put my gear on every game day and join my husband for the ecstasy and the agony of watching the team in action. I have learned a bit about the game and call out the plays or when a player gets sacked.

This is the real beauty of doing something you really don't want to do—you just may learn to enjoy it.

Give them the remote

Okay, this may be more for the guys, so—can your wife occasionally have the remote? Most houses tend to have a remote hog. You know what I mean—the person who wants to be in charge of what everyone should be watching. This would not bother me so much if it meant settling on a program and watching it from beginning to end. What drives me crazy is the surfing.

I just get into the program previously selected and it's changed to something else. I can't figure out if a building is exploding from an attack by a counterintelligence agency or the animals are mating on the Serengeti. It's all a blur.

We have established a "remote calendar" at our house. There are certain nights that I get it and certain nights he gets it. We have a rule that no matter what is chosen by the holder of the remote, that program is what stays on. Not only do we have to accept the decisions, we are not allowed to make a running commentary of why the program choice stinks, how much we hate the actors, and so forth.

We agreed long ago that the TV picks by the remote holder were the rule for the evening. I do wish to note, however, that it is not uncommon for one of us to retire early if he disagrees with the selection.

Iron their clothes

I hate ironing. Most people do. So when I do pull out the board and iron, I figure I may as well do it for a while. Fortunately for me, my husband feels the same way. When we pick up the iron, we both look around for any other item of clothing that may be hanging around and needs a quick touch-up. Here are some tips to make ironing easier:

- Check the tag. It will say whether or not the item can be ironed and what setting to use.
- Fill the iron's water reservoir with distilled water. This will minimize mineral buildup on the iron and on the clothes.
- Put the iron on the right setting. Plug it in and let it sit upright. Wait until it heats up. Many irons have a little light that will go out when the iron has reached the right temperature.
- Start with the coolest settings first if ironing more than one item. It is much faster to heat up the iron than to wait for

it to cool off, and if it's not cool enough the fabric can be ruined.

- Start ironing. Always keep the iron moving; never let it sit still over any part of the garment. If there's a stubborn wrinkle that refuses to iron out, spray some water on it and iron over it with steam. Begin at the big areas and finish with the corners. Once you iron a section, move the garment away from you.

- Hang or fold the garment immediately after ironing. Don't forget to turn off the iron. Some irons now turn off automatically when they aren't used for a period of time.

This favor is especially nice if you know your spouse is a little stressed out. One of you might have a high-profile meeting coming up and really need things perfect. Or you have a special luncheon with little time to organize. Whatever the occasion, having fresh clothes ready is great.

If you are really motivated, finish the ironing for the whole week. Or better yet—buy clothes that don't need to be ironed at all.

Plan and book a vacation

Ah, a nice vacation. What is better? I love to have a vacation or two on the calendar to look forward to. It doesn't need to be fancy or expensive. A simple weekend at a bed and breakfast with a round of golf will do. But it's all the more special if someone else plans it.

This is an easy favor to do and one you will both enjoy. You already know the kinds of things that your spouse likes, so that research is done. Simply coordinate the calendars and then begin looking. The Internet is great for planning a vacation, because it offers about any kind information you need to handle all the details.

There are different approaches to vacation planning based on your preferences. Some folks like to plan every minute down to the last detail, but others like to do more of a free float, letting each day unfold. Still others like to take a theme, such as "tropical," and then plan activities that fit.

You may enjoy a driving vacation. There are dozens of amazing national parks in the U.S. that are relatively cheap to visit and you can easily drive from one to another. For a complete listing of all the parks, check out the official Web site at http://www.nps. gov/index.htm. You can search by name, location, activity, or topic.

A trip to South Dakota is a must for any family. Everyone will enjoy the Badlands and the Black Hills, where you can visit Mount Rushmore. And don't forget Yellowstone and the Tetons, in northwestern Wyoming. The beauty of this area will amaze you.

Here are the Top 10 National Park lodges that you can visit:

1. Ahwahnee Hotel, Yosemite National Park
2. Banff Springs Hotel, Banff National Park, Canada
3. Big Meadows Lodge, Shenandoah National Park
4. Cavallo Point Lodge, Golden Gate National Park
5. Crater Lake Lodge, Crater Lake National Park
6. El Tovar, Grand Canyon National Park
7. Jasper Park Lodge, Jasper National Park, Canada
8. Jenny Lake Lodge, Grand Teton National Park
9. Many Glacier Hotel, Glacier National Park
10. Paradise Inn, Mount Rainier National Park

Whatever your interests, with today's technology, it's easy to organize. Just log on, Google some ideas, and look at what comes up. If you want to make it really special, don't tell your spouse anything about where you are going. Simply explain what to pack and then drive to the airport. This way they learn at the gate where you are heading.

Send them a card for no reason

I know the excuses: "Why should I give the card companies my money?" "All those holidays are just made up by the card companies." "I don't need a card company to say 'I love you.'" Right, right, right.

But you know what? Receiving a card is nice, especially when you aren't expecting it. Funny and unusual cards work well for this purpose. I am always on the lookout for unique cards, and I scoop them up and store them for the next occasion. My husband likes to make his cards on the computer. He inserts pictures, sayings, and love notes that leave me laughing. You can use Microsoft publishing for this purpose and come up with all kinds of ideas.

The placement of your cards can also be creative. Tape one to the steering wheel of the car, or hide one in the suitcase when your spouse is traveling. Cards fit well in briefcases, purses, and notebooks. Clothing offers additional opportunities with pockets, socks, and shoes as ready receptacles. The key here is that your partner does not expect it. Try giving a card for no reason at all, and savor the happy results.

Part II:
Wining and dining

The old saying, "The way to a man's heart is through his stomach," actually applies to most of us. Enjoying good food, wine, or a leisurely drink together is one more way to bond. Most women will tell you that eating a quiet meal with the man they love makes for one of the most intimate moments in their relationship. Eating together improves communication and connection. Happy couples make a point of scheduling time for this culinary connection.

Spending time at the dinner table seems to be good for kids, too. A Harvard Medical School study found the odds of being overweight were 15 percent lower among children who dined with their families most days. Other Harvard research shows that families that dine together eat less fried food and drink less soda. They're also twice as likely to have five servings of fruits and vegetables a day and drink more milk. University of Michigan research showed family meal time was the single strongest predictor of better achievement scores and fewer behavioral problems.[7]

Whether as a family, or just the two of you, make some time to share meals together. Following are some tips to make it happen.

Fix their favorite meal

What a nice surprise after a long day at work and fighting traffic to enter the house and smell your favorite food. Many of us are grateful if anything is planned for dinner, so if it's something we really like to eat—well, that's even better.

Learn what your spouse enjoys eating and make a point to serve it occasionally. Start with a plate of hors d'oeuvres (see below) to begin the relaxation as soon as they walk in. You may even want to set the stage by calling your spouse at work and letting him or her know that there is a surprise for dinner. This will quickly get his or her mind off the outrageous tie the boss is wearing and back to thinking about you.

Shepherd's Pie is one of my husband's favorite meals:

1 lb ground sirloin or lamb

6–8 carrots, sliced into circles

1 can beef broth	fresh mushrooms
1 small onion, chopped	3 tbsp flour
1 bag garlic mashed potatoes	paprika

Preheat oven to 350 degrees. Brown the meat and drain the fat. Add the chopped onion, mushrooms, and carrots and cook until tender. Add the beef broth. Mix the flour in a small amount of cold water and add to the pan. After the gravy thickens, pour into a large sauce dish. Cook and whip the mashed potatoes according to the directions, then spoon potatoes on top of the contents in the sauce dish. Sprinkle on the paprika. Cook for 45 minutes at 350 degrees or until brown on top.

Shish kabobs are one of my favorites:

chunks of sirloin, chicken, or shrimp	teriyaki sauce
green pepper chunks	onion chunks
tomato slices	mushrooms
fruit such as pineapple (optional)	

Marinade the meat or shrimp in the teriyaki sauce overnight. Turn a couple of times to make sure it is coated thoroughly. Cut up the vegetables into square chunks about an inch in diameter. Take wood or metal skewers and start alternating the meat or shrimp with the vegetables or fruit. Cook on the grill, turning frequently until lightly brown. Or broil in the oven, turning until brown. Serve over rice. Take the extra teriyaki sauce, heat it in the microwave, and pour it over the kabob. The nice thing about kabobs is that you can put anything you like on them! If there are other kinds of veggies, or fruit such as pineapple, that you want to add, feel free.

This is also a great time to put out the fancy dishes and eat in the dining room. We have a beautiful dining room with wood panels and stained-glass windows that we forget to use. It seems like too much trouble to set it up "for just us." But, I try to remember that "just us" is who we are and we deserve a little pampering from time to time.

Make sure that you cook extra of the special meal. The leftovers will be delicious the rest of the week.

Make hot chocolate with marshmallows (or whipped cream)

This may not work if you live in Miami, but I live in Wisconsin. We have temperatures in the winter that average 15–20 degrees, but there are times it is much colder. A blizzard with blowing and drifting snow followed by bitter cold with a wind chill at thirty degrees below zero is not uncommon here. After the snow is shoveled off the car and drifts are pushed away from the doors, nothing says "I love you" better than a nice mug of hot chocolate to go.

The basic recipe for hot chocolate is easy: warm some milk, stir in chocolate or cocoa, and top with marshmallows. But you can be a lot more creative by trying variations. For the top twenty recipes for hot chocolate, visit www.allrecipes.com and search for hot chocolate. Favorites like candy cane chocolate, snow flake cocoa, and maple hot chocolate are delicious.

My favorite is Creamy Hot Chocolate:

1 (14-ounce) can sweetened condensed milk
1/2 cup unsweetened cocoa

1 tspn vanilla extract
1/8 tspn salt
6 cups hot water
mini marshmallows

In a large saucepan over medium heat, combine sweetened condensed milk, cocoa, vanilla, and salt; mix well. Slowly stir in the water. Heat through, stirring occasionally. Do not boil. Top with marshmallows (optional). Store covered in refrigerator.

Microwave version:
In a 2-quart glass measuring container, combine all ingredients except the marshmallows. Microwave on high for 2–3 minutes. Top with marshmallows.

Buy special beer

Many of us who enjoy beer have our "standard" brands that we routinely buy. These may include popular brews like Coors, Miller, Bud Light, or something from a local microbrewery. They may not be the cheapest six-packs, but they probably aren't one of the high-end signature brands either. This is why it is fun to occasionally splurge and move up a notch or two.

According to SprecherBrewery.com, here are the 10 best beers in America, with the Web sites where you can find them. Check out some of these fun names.

1. *Dogfish Head 60 Minute IPA*. Dogfish.com. IPA stands for India pale ale, a British style that is traditionally brewed with extra hops and a higher alcohol content, both of which helped preserve the ale on the long journey to the king's beer-guzzling troops in India. These days the bitter, boozy style is one of the most popular in the craft beer world, and 60 Minute IPA is one of the best.

2. *Great Lakes Holy Moses White Ale.* Greatlakesbrewing. com. This is a variation on the Belgian wit, or white, beer, a light, frothy, wheat-based style spiced with coriander and lemon peel. Perfect for a warm spring day.

3. *Full Sail Session Lager.* Fullsailbrewing.com. The words "Session Lager" mean "suitable for drinking for hours on end." This appears to be true. This one has real taste, which makes it all the more likely it will lure you into that long night out.

4. *Smuttynose Big A IPA.* Smuttynose.com. Big A IPA is one of the very few extreme beers that really fulfills the promise that beers make: to deliver more of what you like without messing it up.

5. *Great Lakes Burning River Pale Ale.* Greatlakesbrewery. com. "Burning River" is a great name; unfortunately it is a reference to the worst days of the Cuyahoga River, a waterway once so damaged by coal plants on its banks that it periodically caught fire. Not to worry, there is no oil slick in this beer.

6. *Samuel Adams Black Lager.* Samueladams.com. Tired of hearing your in-laws complain that dark beers are "just too heavy"? Try this black lager from microbrewing trail-blazer Jim Koch's Boston Beer Company. It's smooth and dark, but not too filling.

7. *Sprecher Hefe Weiss.* Sprecherbrewery.com. My home-town, Milwaukee, was once called the Beer Capital of the World, thanks to the breweries cranking out Pabst, Schlitz, and Miller. Sprecher guards a more authentic strain of the city's brewing tradition with its perfectly crafted German-style beers.

8. *Deschutes Broken Top Bock.* Deschutesbrewery.com. This German-style beer is called "bock" because it's named

after the town where it was born, Einbeck. It has rich, roasted malt flavors and tangy Eastern European hops.

9. *Jolly Pumpkin Bam Biere.* Jollypumpkin.com. This one is an acquired taste. "Brett," as it's sometimes called, is often described as leathery or earthy (a flavor sometimes referred to as "horse blanket"). This one isn't for everyone.

10. *New Glarus Yokel.* Newglarusbrewing.com. This Wisconsin company produces delicious rustic lager that rivals the best breweries in Germany.

Choose a specialty beer the next time you want to try something new. There are lots of great options.

chicken broth and wine. You are supposed to use just a cup or two of the cooking wine, but I dump the whole bottle in and have never had any complaints. Cook until tender. About twenty minutes before you serve, add a little flour mixed into cold water and stir into the gravy to thicken. Serve with wild rice.

Add a salad and some wine and you have a great dinner. Coq au Vin is even better the second day as the garlic works through the sauce with the other spices. This recipe was given to me by one of my bridesmaids, Wanda, at my wedding. I have been making Coq au Vin ever since.

Fight with your spouse? Make Coq au Vin. Sick friend? Coq au Vin to the rescue. Want to impress the new boss? Coq au Vin for dinner. It simply has magical qualities.

Now, of course, you may have your own special dish, but I highly suggest that you try this one. I guarantee you that it will impress your partner.

Dine at a fancy restaurant

As long as we are talking about food, what about a nice meal out? Granted, a fancy restaurant isn't affordable every night for most of us. But that is exactly what makes it so special. Rather than the $5.99 fish fry we usually grab on a Friday night, a trip to a fancy venue is a nice change from plastic baskets lined with waxed paper. And you don't have to mortgage the house to do it.

It's possible to go to very nice places and still find an economical dinner. Here are a few ideas to hold down your bill:

- Eat a healthy snack before you go out. This will stop you from arriving at the restaurant in a ravenous state ready to order too much food.
- Order something that takes time to eat. This will slow down your eating so that you feel full before you fill up the table with foods. Plates of cheeses, olives, or salad work well for this purpose.
- Order appetizers as your meal. They often are more than

enough to fill you up. We may order two or three different options and then share them.

- Watch what you drink. This is where restaurants really make their money. At an upscale restaurant, you can pay $10 or more for a simple drink. The popular "designer" drinks can cost even more. Have a nightcap when you get home and you will save a lot of money.
- Order in sequence. Order and eat your appetizer before you place your order for an entrée. When you order everything at the same time, it's easy to order much more food than you really want.
- Share food. Supersizing has hit most of the food industry and portions are often enormous. Consider splitting an entrée and then just paying for an extra salad or soup.
- Take food home. We often take half of our entrées home for lunches the next day. Sometimes, we even get another complete dinner out of them. Then the meal is really cost-effective.
- Skip (or share) dessert. Desserts add to the bill and pack on the calories. Skip it entirely or just get a small portion to share.

A nice restaurant gives both of you an excuse to dress up and put a little effort into the evening. With a spritz of cologne and some favorite music on the iPod in the car, you set the mood for talking, flirting, and connecting.

When we go, we like to move slowly. It is an event, not just a meal. We like to linger over a drink, order appetizers, and enjoy the main course. We are not big dessert eaters, but occasionally we will split something with some decaf coffee.

The point is, we are out together, talking. No one is watching TV or reading the paper at the table. And if it takes a few bucks to make this happen, it is well worth it. On a nice night, we may top off the evening by taking a walk in the park or just sitting on the deck.

We have made it a ritual always to go to a fancy restaurant for our anniversary. In the early years, we really had to save to make this happen. We would always say that we couldn't afford to do it, but we went anyway. Funny, after nearly thirty years we still say we can't afford it. I think we're just broke at a higher level.

Make mimosas for Sunday brunch

A mimosa is a cocktail-like drink composed of one part champagne and one part thoroughly chilled orange juice. It is traditionally served in a tall champagne flute for a morning brunch or to guests at a wedding or other event.

The origins of the mimosa are somewhat murky. Some claim the drink was invented at the Paris Ritz in 1924. It is similar to another cocktail, the Buck's Fizz, which was introduced in England in 1921, and named after a club where it was first served. The Buck's Fizz is traditionally made with champagne and orange juice, although grenadine is sometimes added to the mixture. Outside the United States, the mixture of orange juice and champagne is referred to as a Buck's Fizz, while the term "mimosa," regardless of its origins, is used in the U.S.

There is agreement that both the champagne and the orange juice should be chilled, but the exact proportions are often debated. Some recipes call for a measurement of three parts champagne to one part orange juice, while others prefer a half-and-half ratio. I suppose it depends on how much of a morning buzz you would like.

We make ours half and half and serve them with a twist of orange on the side. This feels so New York and they complement a lazy Sunday brunch. Make sure that you get some nice glass flutes to add to the elegance and enjoy the sparkle.

Clean the grill

Well, this sounds romantic, doesn't it? But it is such a nasty job, your spouse will definitely appreciate your efforts here, especially if it is viewed as that person's job. It doesn't have to be as hard as it seems. A clean grill burns better and doesn't leave a bad taste on food. Here's how to make it easy.

Remove cooking grates and set them in warm soapy water to soak. If it's a charcoal grill, then remove the coal grate and brush out the insides. If it's a gas grill, remove briquettes, lava rocks, or the metal flame shield to expose the burner. Clean out ash and residue from around the burner, careful to make sure the burner is in the correct place when you are done. Use a stiff wire brush and a little soapy water to gently scrub the inside surfaces of the grill. Remove any particles from the grill and re-assemble. For a gas grill, brush off briquettes or lava rocks or wash the metal flame shield in warm soapy water. Remove the cooking grates from the water and brush clean with the wire brush. Coat inside surfaces and cooking grates with cooking oil or spray. Put grates back on the grill. Allow the whole grill to air dry. Allow an extra five minutes of heating time the next time you grill to make sure any cleaning residue has burned off.

Make sure you have the rest of the grilling supplies on hand. If you have a gas grill, fill up the tank. If you use charcoal, have an extra bag on hand.

While most of us grill hamburger, chicken, or steak, there are many other things that work well for grilling. Try vegetables, kabobs, seafood, or even a turkey. Just fire it up and then relax with a lemonade and talk.

We grill out all summer long—things just taste better off the grill.

Serve hors d'oeuvres (appetizers)

Hors d'oeuvres are great and not just for company. It is fun to put together a quick tray of cut-up vegetables, dip, olives, cheese, and crackers to nibble on when the two of you regroup at home. It is also a great excuse to get out the glass, sectioned tray that you got as a wedding present from your great-aunt.

One of my favorite treats is fresh guacamole served with gourmet chips. Here is an easy recipe:

3 Hass avocados, halved, seeded, and peeled
1 lime, juiced
1 tspn kosher salt or sea salt
1 tspn ground cumin
1 tspn cayenne
1 medium onion, diced
2 Roma tomatoes, seeded and diced
1 tbsp chopped cilantro
1 clove garlic, minced

In a large bowl, place the scooped avocado pulp and lime juice, then toss to coat. Drain and reserve the lime juice, after all the avocados have been coated. Using a potato masher, add the salt, cumin, and cayenne, and mash. Then, fold in the onions, tomatoes, cilantro, and garlic. Add one tablespoon of the reserved lime juice. Let sit at room temperature for one hour and then serve.

I like to put out hors d'oeuvres and make some fresh lemonade, just to sit and talk when we get home from work.

I can still remember the first time I did it. My husband walked in, looked around, and asked who was coming to dinner. Then my daughter told me, "You have too much time on your hands." Sigh.

Eat on the deck or patio

It's a little extra work to set the table on the deck, but it is so worthwhile. Now, I'm not talking about paper plates and plastic cups—that's called a picnic. I'm talking about nice place settings with some flowers to decorate.

I find that when we get out of the kitchen and the house, we talk more. Pretty soon we are talking events at work, what is in the news, or how our accident-prone neighbor is perched precariously on a ladder to repair the gutter.

Sometimes we sit and talk about nothing. We swap stories from the past and tell of embarrassing moments. One of our favorite verbal games is, "Tell me something you never mentioned before." This is increasingly difficult the longer you are together. It forces you to dig deep into the crevices in your brain to think of an incident or event you never shared. It can be very funny and full of surprises. For example, I didn't know that my husband burned down his garage as a kid.

You can also ask each other questions. It may feel a little silly at first, but fun and laughter are the goal. Here are some suggestions:

- What is the most embarrassing thing that ever happened to you?
- Do you have a secret ambition?
- Where is someplace you have always wanted to go?
- Name someone that you truly admire.
- Name something in your childhood that was most precious to you.
- How do you like your steak cooked?
- Who would you like to have dinner with (dead or alive)?
- What is your favorite form of exercise?
- Where do you go to get away from it all?
- Where is your favorite vacation spot?
- What is the worst thing that could happen to you?
- What were you wearing when we met?
- What relaxes you?
- What is your favorite flower?
- What is your favorite color?
- What are the names of your best friends?
- What is your favorite music group or artist?
- What is your ideal romantic evening?

Get outside and enjoy the weather.

Put out the fancy dishes

Perhaps you have noticed that you "save" your guest towels, "save" the silverware, and "save" the fancy dishes for important visitors. Well, stop saving. You really don't need an excuse to set out the nice china, silverware, and cloth napkins. Use them anytime you want to take an ordinary meal and spice it up.

You don't have fancy dishes? Then go buy them. I find really nice dishes for cheap at some of the local department stores. They often go on closeout and you can stock up, preparing for the inevitable chips and nicks. It doesn't have to be china, just "fancy."

There are now plates in all different shapes and sizes. Skip the boring round ones and look for square, wavy, or triangles. Find the bright colors and outrageous patterns to create a really fun table.

Keep your eyes open at Kohl's, Target, and other discount stores. I sometimes pick up new plates for as little as a couple of bucks a piece. At that price, I don't care if one gets chipped or broken.

Celebrate their birthday

Birthdays are fun and a great excuse for a celebration. While some argue that birthdays are just for kids, I beg to differ. I think birthdays are really more fun the older you get.

Consider a "theme" birthday based on one of your spouse's interests. He likes golf? Buy him some new stuff like golf balls, a towel, or GPS system. Book a golf weekend for the two of you and have the hotel deliver some fresh cheesecake.

She likes shopping? Book a bed and breakfast in a quaint town with lots of shops and spend some time together. If you can't stand shopping, you can watch the movie channel while she uses your charge card.

The "big" birthdays—30, 40, 50, 60—demand extra attention. The black balloons and gifts of Grecian Formula are old gags. It's much more fun to plan a party or a vacation. This might be the time that you save some extra money and take the trip you have always dreamed of.

Some folks like surprise parties, but check this out long before you plan one. I, for one, can hardly think of anything more dreadful. Too often, you end up with a multigenerational party where people really don't know one another. You end up spending all your time trying to make sure that everyone is included and having a good time. This can be a lot of work without a lot of laughs. I would much rather be out with a few of my close friends.

Part III:
Touching and connecting

Marriage is sometimes more about flannel nightgowns and snore strips than physical affection. But little gestures can rekindle the flames of passion. It just takes a little effort.

I know, you want things spontaneous, the way they were when you first met. I hear that all the time. But really, what was spontaneous about it? Most of us would spend a good part of the day preparing for a date; showering, shaving, brushing our teeth, picking out clothes, and putting on cologne. Then we flirted like crazy over dinner or at a movie, until "spontaneous" romance just happened.

One of the challenges of marriage is that stability and routine can also be boring. We stop putting the effort into wooing our partner, because all we need do is just roll over in bed, and "whoosh," they are available beside us. But a little attention can make things a lot more exciting. Shake it up by trying some of these tips.

Mist the bed with a scented spray

This one might be just for the gal, as I can't really see a guy going out to purchase mist spray. I don't want to sound cynical, but I doubt my husband would (a) know where to buy it or (b) even know what it is for. I suspect that most guys are in a similar boat.

That doesn't mean that they don't appreciate a nice-smelling bed. Pulling back the covers and smelling lilacs or orange peel can be fun and exciting. While women tend to get turned on by "emotional connection," like talking together, men tend to get turned on by their senses—what they see, smell, and touch.

There are lots of products that can fill this bill. A good place to look is Bath and Body Works, which carries bed mist in many fragrances designed to soothe and relax you. Also check out Bed-BathandBeyond.com, which has a large catalog of mists for your bed and pillow.

If you do try misting the bed, make sure not to overdo it. The first time I put this idea to the test, I sprayed "lilac" all over the bed, pillows, and covers. As my husband ascended the stairs, he began to cough and couldn't stop. He eventually had to sleep in the other bedroom. Sigh. Nowadays I spritz no more than a dab here and there.

Say "I love you"
at least once every day

This one really isn't all that hard. Yet, too often we are stingy in saying "I love you" to the people we care about. At our house, we finish most of our phone conversations with a quick "I love you" before hanging up. But you can also say it when it isn't automatic or expected. Practice saying "I love you" when your partner least expects it.

You can use this phrase when you find your gas tank filled, dinner made, or your clothes washed and ironed. You can use it for absolutely no reason at all. Just look at your spouse and say, "I love you."

I hear the same story all the time. Someone dies and his loved one says, "I never told him how much I loved him." What? Where have you been? Why not? "I love you's" are just too easy to do.

Touch them while they are driving

Although you certainly don't want to distract your partner from the task at hand, it is a loving gesture to have some kind of physical contact while in the car. This can be your hand on his leg, putting your arm around her shoulder, or twirling his hair. If you were still dating, this would be called flirting. How nice is that?

Especially on a long trip, it is nice to settle into the car and set the mood. Pack up your iPod with your favorite music and plug it into the car stereo. Apple sells adaptors for this purpose that will scan for an empty channel automatically, and then indicate where to program the radio. Hit play and crank up the tunes.

Of course this is an excellent opportunity to demonstrate your skills at singing along, dancing, or playing air guitar. In between "takes," you can lovingly caress the driver.

Spoon in bed

This favorite cuddling position can be used anytime, but it is especially nice during winter when the sheets are cold. With your spouse on their side with legs slightly bent, you cuddle up behind in exactly the same position. Named after the way spoons fit into the silverware drawer, it's very snuggly and warm. I like to throw my arm around as well for a really tight fit.

Spooning communicates a range of emotions, sometimes more quickly and accurately than words. In a series of experiments led by Matthew Hertenstein, a psychologist at DePauw University in Indiana, volunteers were asked to communicate emotions through touching a blindfolded stranger. The participants were able to communicate eight distinct emotions, from gratitude to disgust to love, and some did so with about 70 percent accuracy.

A warm touch seems to set off the release of oxytocin, which helps create a sensation of trust. This helps the prefrontal areas of the brain, which help regulate emotion, to relax. This frees the brain up for its primary purpose: problem solving. In effect, the body interprets a supportive touch as meaning "I'll share the load." It may be that humans build relationships precisely for this reason, according to James A. Coan, a psychologist at the University of Virginia. "We are wired to literally share the processing load, and this is the signal we're getting when we receive support through touch."[8]

Maybe AT&T had the right idea when they said "reach out and touch someone."

Play footsie under the table

This is a fun one that can be done at any meal or gathering. I think it's especially fun when there is a table of friends or relatives and you two can be a bit sneaky.

Sit at a table next to or across from your partner. Your feet should be able to come in direct contact with the other's, without anyone else's feet getting in the way. (It could be very embarrassing to "footsie" the wrong person!) Remove your shoe, and run your foot up to their calf and knee. Tap or push their foot lightly and playfully, then pull away. Do it just once and see how they react. If they pull their feet quickly out of reach, you may want to consider the timing. If he looks around smiling, you know the game is on. Look away as if you are totally innocent. Nudge her feet again, this time a little more firmly and for a longer time. If she starts to nudge back, you can give a playful smile or maybe raise your eyebrows to further flirt. Tangle up your feet with his. This can include massaging an ankle with the sole of your foot and locking ankles (twisting your ankle around his). Keep making eye contact and smiling.

If you want to get naughty, you can also use your foot to tease and tickle. Like fooling around in church, it's all the funnier because you both are trying to keep a straight face. I like to play this game until it's clear my husband is getting annoyed or someone is about to notice.

Rub your partner's back without being asked

The key to this one is "not being asked." Just start rubbing your partner's back as he begins to fall asleep and let him know that you will help him relax. The key to a great back rub is to repeat motions that are slow and deep. Here are some tips to get you started:

- Using the heels of your hands, execute a long stroke, starting from the pelvis and going up both sides of the spine.
- When you get to the shoulders, swivel your hands so that your fingers reach out to the ribs, and stroke back down again. Repeat this maneuver several times.
- If desired, you may also put lotion on to make the motions more smooth and comfortable.
- Work your thumbs in small, deep circles, starting in the interior part of the shoulder blades, moving up the spine into the base of the head and then down to the small of the back.
- At the base of the head, deeply press the tips of your forefin-

ger and middle finger into the neck area. Alternate hands, overlapping your strokes as you glide down.

Take your time and enjoy the contact. Maybe the next night you can reverse roles.

Let your spouse pick out your perfume or cologne

It really surprised me the first time my husband bought me cologne. I thought to myself, "He really has no right to pick out what fragrance I want to wear." But the more I thought about it, the more it began to make sense. After all, he was the one smelling it. You really don't smell your own fragrance after you wear it for a while. He clearly had an opinion about this issue, and as I quickly discovered, so do I.

I hate the scent of cheap cologne or perfume. It hangs in the air around the wearer like a heavy fog. Really nice options are available without huge price tags. Here are the top five perfumes and colognes according to Scentiments.com:

Perfumes
1. Michael Kors
2. D & G—La Lune
3. Jo Malone

4. Miller Harris
5. Issey Miyake

Colognes
1. Acqua Di Gio by Giorgio Armani
2. Ed Hardy by Christian Audigie
3. Cool Water by Davidoff
4. Paul Sebastian
5. Curve by Liz Claiborne

Go shopping together and pick out one of the nicer fragrances. They can be powerful aphrodisiacs.

Do long hugs

Everybody loves a hug, but long ones are even better. The kind of hug where you just hang like drapery on your partner's body, let time slow down, and breathe together is a special gift. You both linger just a bit longer than usual and then realize it is a great place to be. Long hugs are not only great, they may also be good for your health.

A team from the University of North Carolina studied the effects of hugging on both men and women in thirty-eight couples. The study showed hugs increased levels of oxytocin, a "bonding" hormone, and reduced blood pressure, which cuts the risk of heart disease.[9] People need human touch and hugs are a great delivery system.

Hugs are not only good for you, they're fun too! There is no reason to be stingy. Some of the best hugs are given for no reason at all. A good "hug habit" is to always hug hello and hug good-bye, with a nice long embrace before bedtime. Some couples hug together until they fall asleep. Others embrace on the couch while they watch TV.

Whatever your hugging style, practice lingering awhile and loving each other.

Give your partner a foot massage

Feet really get a bad rap. Most of us abuse them, don't appreciate them, and give them minimal maintenance. Yet, feet are one of the most sensual parts of your body. They contain a lot of nerve endings, and a good foot massage tends to relax not just your feet but your whole body. This is why a lot of us pay to get pedicures—because they include a foot massage.

It takes very little effort or knowledge to give a good foot massage because most people just love having their feet touched and caressed, particularly when they are sore or aching. Grab some towels and some massage oil or lotion. Sorbolene cream or another lotion will do the trick. Start by oiling up the foot and giving it a general all-over rub with the palms of your hands. Conduct a little foot manipulation. Hold the heel firm with one hand, and with the other, gently hold and twist the forefoot clockwise and counterclockwise. Manipulate the toes, each in turn, up and down, left and right, and follow by massaging and caressing deep in between the toes. Massage in small circles on the soles of the feet with the thumbs followed by kneading using the fingers, heel of the palm, or knuckles. Now, this move is a bit tricky. Grab the foot like a hamburger, toes facing you, fingers on top, thumbs on bottom under the balls of the feet. Manipulate the joints at the balls of the feet by lifting each joint independently up and down. Massage the top of the foot using the palm or the fingertips. Use your knuckles on the underside of the foot, especially kneading the arch. Finish with another all-over rub and then start on the other foot.

If you learn and practice how to give a foot massage using this technique, you will be a real hit with your spouse. Remember the more you practice, the better you'll get, and the happier the receiver will be!

Hold hands at the movies

I love couples who hold hands. Sometimes you spot them in the park, at a movie, or just walking down the street. They may be swinging their arms or just gently holding each other. It is a gesture not limited to the young. Few things are more endearing than an elderly couple who still hold hands.

If you haven't generally been a hand holder, the movies are a good place to start. Just reach across and grab your spouse's hand. You can give a light squeeze and then rest both hands on the arm-rest or one of your laps.

Holding hands is especially fun at a scary movie, because you can give your partner a vice-like grip when the scenes get tense, or try to jump in their lap. If you are looking for films that offer this opportunity, here are the top 10 scariest movies I have seen:

10. *A Simple Plan (1988).* With Bill Paxton, Bridget Fonda, and Billy Bob Thornton, this movie is full of suspense and intrigue. Two brothers and a friend find $4 million

in the cockpit of a downed plane and make a series of decisions that change everyone's life. If you are a Billy Bob fan, you will love this film.

9. *The Shining (1980).* Jack Nicholson is superb as a psychotic killer in this Stephen King thriller. The inspiration for the movie came from King's visit to the Stanley Hotel in Estes Park, Colorado. Ever since I saw this movie, Nicholson always looks a bit crazy to me.

8. *Halloween (1978).* This film by John Carpenter relies on suspense rather than sensationalism. Our fear is caused by what might happen rather than actual events, as the viewer spends a good amount of time in darkness, seeing things that may or may not be there. Jamie Lee Curtis is great as a terrorized teen.

7. *Terminator 2: Judgment Day (1991).* The Arnold (Arnold Schwarzenegger) is at the top of his game with this sci-fi classic. The special effects are still amazing after twenty years and the plot is intriguing.

6. *The Texas Chainsaw Massacre (1974).* A group of annoying teens makes a wrong turn on a road trip through Texas and encounters the most dysfunctional family imaginable. It's a teen exploitation flick shot like a documentary. A film filled with gore.

5. *Westworld (1973).* "Have we got a vacation for you!" John Blane, played by James Brolin, visits a futuristic theme park, where androids run amok and a gunslinger (Yul Brynner) packs a pistol filled with real bullets. The possibility that the android will prevail provides nonstop, heart-pounding suspense.

4. *Invasion of the Body Snatchers (1978).* In San Francisco, a group of people discover that the human race is being replaced one by one by clones. Starring Donald Sutherland

and Brooke Adams. Jeff Goldblum also turns up in one of his early roles.

3. *Night of the Living Dead (1968)*. A group of kids get trapped inside a farmhouse by an endless stream of flesh-eating zombies. If you are a zombie lover, this is a must-see. You may also want to read *The Zombie Guide—Complete Protection from the Living Dead* to fully understand what zombies are capable of. There is no hope here, only suffocating terror.

2. *Repulsion (1965)*. Director Roman Polanski did more horror afterward, with *Rosemary's Baby* and *The Tenant*, but this is a menacing, nightmarish profile of one woman's descent into madness. The film is nearly silent, creating a mounting mood of dread.

1. *Psycho (1960)*. More than just a film, Alfred Hitchcock's *Psycho* was a cultural slap in the face. Censors wanted to ban it, while screaming audiences couldn't get enough of it. To this day, I have difficulty taking a shower at a hotel.

Pick up one of these today and snuggle in with your partner and a bowl of popcorn.

Wear something provocative

You may view this tip as something just for women, but men can dress a little sexy from time to time, as well. As a general rule, partly clothed is sexier than completely nude. People like to be teased—they like to guess. This is why magazines photograph the stars with peek-a-boo tops and low-cut gowns.

It takes more confidence and a stronger self-image to dress provocatively in front of your spouse than it does to dress sassy in public. To dress immodestly in public is fairly easy. You get lots of attention without having to "do" anything to follow through on it.

To dress provocatively at home or "in the bedroom" generally means that the clothing is ultimately going to come off. Feeling sexy means you like and accept yourself—complete with flaws and imperfections. You are comfortable in your own skin. Being at peace with oneself is the key to unlocking one's sexual potential in marriage.

You can be the star at your own home. Have some clothes, pajamas, or T-shirts that are just for the two of you. Wear them around the house after dinner when you are ready to relax. It makes it easy for her to snuggle up. You can also dress a bit sassy for going out. Many of the styles for women include lower-cut, tighter tops that were once found only in Europe. It is generally acceptable to wear many of these styles regardless of your age.

Buy some new clothes and have some fun.

Do unexpected sexual favors

There is an old joke that if you put a dollar in a jar every time you have sex the first year of marriage, and take a dollar out of the jar for every sexual interlude after the first year, you will never empty the jar.

While people joke about sex in marriage, married folks seem to be a great deal more satisfied with their sex lives than single people, even though the actual act may be of shorter duration. According to a national sex survey of 3,400 Americans conducted by researchers at the University of Chicago, almost 30 percent of women who don't live with a male partner indicate that sex often lasts for more than an hour. For live-in partners, only 13 percent of the women, and only 8 percent of wives, reported this. Almost three-quarters of married women reported that lovemaking lasted fifteen to sixty minutes, with 16 percent finishing even faster.[10]

But shorter appears to be sweeter. Not only do married people report that they feel emotionally fulfilled, they also report the highest levels of physical pleasure. Rather than finding monogamy monotonous, 91 percent of husbands and wives say that they are "thrilled" with their sex lives. According to the survey, 42 percent of married women said they found sex extremely emotionally and physically satisfying, compared with just 31 percent of single women who had a sex partner. And 50 percent of married men find sex physically satisfying, compared to 39 percent of cohabitating men.

Married couples seem to fall into a pattern of predictability that is satisfying and fun, but that doesn't mean you can't spice it up from time to time. Surprise your partner with something new or a sexual favor you know that they will love. Use oils and other products to increase sensation and touch. Whisper sexy statements in their ear and let them know how much fun they are.

This extra effort will further increase your connection both in the bedroom and out.

Learn how to pole dance

Okay, this one is a little strange. I was working on this book while waiting for dinner in a restaurant. When the waitress noticed what I was working on, I asked her for suggestions. After consulting with the kitchen staff, this was the tip they offered. I think it's cute. Indeed, one way to improve your marriage is to do something unexpected and stimulating.

There is a great scene in the movie *Fried Green Tomatoes*, a 1991 film based on the novel *Fried Green Tomatoes at the Whistle Stop Cafe* by Fannie Flagg. Starring Kathy Bates, Jessica Tandy, Mary-Louise Parker, and Mary Stuart Masterson, it tells the story of a Depression-era friendship between two women, Ruth and Idgie, and a 1980s friendship between Evelyn (Kathy Bates) and Ninny (Jessica Tandy), an elderly woman who knew Ruth and Idgie.

A subplot in the movie is Evelyn's dissatisfaction with her marriage and life and her attempts to improve both. One evening, she opens the door for her husband wrapped in nothing but plastic wrap. Thinking she will get his attention, she is shocked when he walks right past her and asks, "What's for dinner?" Standing there dumbfounded at his lack of surprise, she becomes determined to take control of her own destiny.

Wrapping up in plastic wrap failed in the movie but, trust me, most men would notice. And they will certainly notice if you install a pole and learn to dance!

Join your spouse in the shower

Don't wait to be asked, just step in nude. I guarantee that they won't ask you to leave. Couples who shower together can create a level of closeness that is intimate and playful. Many couples enjoy showering together without its being sexual.

Turn off the lights and light a candle or two. There are now "flameless" candles that run on batteries and look very close to the real ones without the danger or inconvenience of fire or wax dripping all over the place. Put on soft music that you both enjoy. Bring an assortment of soaps and lathers so that you can pamper each other. Take turns soaping each other up and teasing a bit.

If you have a standard shower (3 feet by 3 feet), you will have to take turns as to who gets the majority of the water from the shower head. This can be very annoying and quickly turn a romantic moment into a confrontation over the water flow. The new low-flow shower heads that are being installed across the country can make showering together even more of a challenge as they sometimes produce only a trickle of water.

There is a trend, however, to update bathrooms into a luxurious room of the house. New homes and remodeling projects are turning bathrooms into home spas where one can retreat in solitude. Shower stalls are being enlarged and may include multiple body sprays in addition to the main showerhead. This way, no one is standing out in the cold. Standard tubs are being replaced with whirlpool or bubble massage for real relaxation.

If you get an opportunity to remodel a bathroom, I highly recommend looking into these upgrades. You can add four body sprays to your shower for around $550. Install a faucet that has multiple settings and you can control the water stream in every direction. If you are looking for ideas for your new bathroom, check out Kohler.com.

Part IV: Playing together

Playing together gives you things to talk and laugh about. Couples with strong marriages recognize that activities may change over the years, but commitment to discovering them together does not. As partners, they are open to trying new things and having new experiences, and they laugh together even when everything seems to go wrong.

Too many of us forget how to play once we are grown. Play comes naturally to children and can be as simple as catching fireflies, playing tag, or pretending. But somewhere in the process of becoming responsible, play can get lost.

There is considerable research that adults also need to play; for their health, their minds, and their sanity. When you take time to do something you love, levels of dopamine and serotonin rise in your body, which makes you feel calm and pleasant. Playing together also gives you a chance to connect, reflect inwardly, learn a new skill, relax and de-stress, and increase your creativity. Play unleashes energy, and this energy flows into your marriage.

Couples frequently insist that they do not have the money to spend time playing together. But there are many activities that do not cost a lot of money, such as walks in the park, coffee on the patio, or a budget movie. The key is to keep a sense of adventure alive in your marriage so that life is fun. Following are some suggestions.

Play games they like to play

This may mean games that they win. A friend of mine frequently plays board games with her husband. After a time, she noticed that he always seemed to win. When she asked him how this was possible, he responded, "I only play games that I win." Well, that explains it.

But playing games is fun. To make it fair, have some games you are both good at. Try board games, card games, and group games. Here are some of our favorite games:

- Monopoly. Perhaps the best known of all modern board games, Monopoly has been around since 1933. From the joy of watching your partner go to jail to snagging Boardwalk early in the game, this game is fun and easy to play. This is a solid game involving basic economics.
- Mah-jongg. Talk about old games, mah-jongg has roots that stretch back to about a.d. 800. It is a game of skill,

strategy, and calculation that involves a certain degree of chance. This creates surprises and frequent turns on the way to a victory.

- Scrabble. The most popular word game in the world, the deluxe edition boasts several worthwhile features, including a board that spins and holds letters in place. Sometimes we make up words just to see if the other player is paying attention.

- Backgammon. Backgammon is the race game you might not even realize is a race game. The goal is to get all of your pieces off the board before your opponent does the same. While you need skill, luck is also your best friend for this one.

- Battleship. Two players secretly deploy their navies and then try to sink the other's ships. A simple game, it is entertaining and easy to play.

- Stratego. Deploy your armies in a way that protects your flag while giving you a chance to capture your opponent's flag. Strategy and intrigue lead to healthy and humorous confrontations.

- Checkers. This board game can be played anywhere and is easy to set up. There are also travel editions to keep you both occupied on long flights or trips.

- Chess. From the seventh century up to today, the rules of chess have evolved. It's still a wonderful game of strategy and skill that you can play together.

- There are also thousands of card games that you two can play together. Here are three favorites to try out:

- Golf. We love this card game. You play nine "holes," trying to get the lowest score you possibly can. Jokers are a minus 3, so there are often friendly battles over these cards. We keep packs of cards handy when we travel, since the game can be played anywhere.

- Cribbage (crib). Crib can be played with more than two people, but I prefer it one on one. In addition to a deck of cards you'll need a cribbage board, which is part of what makes this game unique.
- Gin rummy. Gin uses a standard deck of 52 cards and is all about action. There are a lot of things going on and you can totally lose yourself in this game.

Surprise them with a water balloon

Water balloon wars are a continuing favorite at my house. It works best, of course, if you have a balcony or porch where you can drop them suddenly on the unaware below. This can set off a battle that can last several hours until everyone is soaked.

You need very little equipment to begin a water balloon scrimmage. Just buy balloons, stretch them around a water faucet, and fill them until comfortably full. Do not overfill or you risk a premature burst in your lap. This procedure, however, can get tedious if you plan to create an ammunition arsenal.

For only a few bucks, you can buy balloons that come with an attachment, which fits over the faucet and makes filling them a lot easier. We routinely use this attachment if we want to build an arsenal. You can also get creative with the execution and launch. Water balloon launcher slingshots are available on Amazon and at other stores.

On waterballoonlaunchers.com, you can buy the "Beast," which is touted as the biggest launcher out there. The latex tubing is as big around as your thumb and the launch pad is a whopping 10 inches x 10 inches. This launcher can hurl balloons an eighth of a mile. There are also water balloon cannons and single-person launchers that can make any "war" a lot of fun.

Step up to advanced weaponry by purchasing a balloon bazooka. At balloonbazooka.com, they boast a basic unit that can launch a balloon more than 300 feet. It has a small air tank that can launch up to twelve balloons at once.

Check out these sites, stock up on equipment, and let the war begin.

Buy tickets to their favorite rock group

My husband loves the Rolling Stones. I keep telling him that he is stuck in the 1960s, but he doesn't care. He loves the old rock and roll music. So when the Stones set out with their "Bigger Bang" tour, I went online and got tickets. This was no small feat.

The Rolling Stones are excellent businessmen and marketers. To get tickets, you have to join their Fan Club, which costs $100 a year. Once a fan club member, you can buy the tickets when they go on "pre-sale." In reality, this is the only way you will get tickets because once they actually go "on sale" they are sold out.

As soon as I heard about the tour, I logged on and joined the Fan Club (I also get a discount on their overpriced merchandise). I bought great seats and enclosed them in a card for our twenty-fifth anniversary.

To celebrate the event we made reservations at an expensive restaurant downtown. As we sat down to have a cocktail, I handed Charlie the card. When he opened it up and saw the tickets, he yelled in delight, much to the annoyance of the other diners. With everyone looking at him, he explained in a wavy voice, "She got me Rolling Stones tickets!"

No one cared. But he did. He had wanted to see them his entire life.

The night of the concert, we arrived early to enjoy the ambiance and people watching. As the lights dimmed and Mick Jagger pranced around the stage, my husband was all smiles. Much to my surprise, I also thought it was the best concert that I ever attended.

About midway through the concert, the entire stage moved on tracks across the room to the other side of the arena so that everyone in attendance could get a close view of the action. How fun is that?

We were both thrilled for three hours and my husband still talks about it. I got a lot of points for this one.

Dance in the living room

When we first got married, we could not afford to go out. Renting a movie was about as frisky as we could get. But one night, my husband put music on the stereo, put a red lightbulb in the lamp, and asked me to dance. With music blaring, we danced until we were out of breath and laughing. Over the next few years, we danced more and more. We danced at weddings, at fish fries, and at parties. We danced in the moonlight on the deck and at the festival across the street. We danced at weekly ballroom lessons. In short, we became dancing maniacs.

All this dancing helped us in a number of ways. We found we had to work and practice together. To create a smooth dance pattern, we were forced to communicate with one leading and one following. I still remember our first dance teacher, who told me, "Worse than a wallflower, worse than a weed, is a determined woman who wants to lead." Sigh.

Dancing together creates another way for the two of you to connect. Focused on the details at first, you quickly learn how to move together without even thinking about the next step. Couples who do this well find that their bodies begin to synchronize into new movements. Holding, touching, and moving to the music is the most romantic skill any couple can add to their married life.

Dancing is also great exercise. Depending on the step, ballroom dancing can burn anywhere from 250 to 400 calories an hour—about the same as a brisk half-hour walk. More demanding dances like the salsa, cha-cha, or disco can be the same as an intense workout.

An activity that is both romantic and helps you lose weight? Priceless. I hope that my husband and I are still dancing together when we are ninety.

Laugh at their jokes

I know, "what if they aren't funny?" Laugh anyway. Everyone loves to be the comedian at times, and a spouse is the perfect audience. Listen to the stories, even if you have heard them before. Stare at your spouse with rapt attention and then let out the loudest belly laugh you can muster. Yes, he will think that he is Mr. Saturday Night Live, but so what? It's fun.

An interesting thing about humor is that it tends to be contagious. The more you two laugh and joke together, the funnier things will seem. Perhaps you have had the experience of staying up late with a group of friends telling stories. Pretty soon, everything that is said is funny.

Start the laughter at your house with the top five jokes, according to *Readers Digest*:

Crime and Punishment. A man, shocked by how his buddy is dressed, asks him, "How long have you been wearing a bra?" The friend replies, "Ever since my wife found it in the glove compartment."

Vow of Silence. Every ten years, the monks in the monastery are allowed to break their vow of silence to speak two words. Ten years go by and it's one monk's first chance. He thinks for a second before saying, "Food bad." Ten years later, he says, "Bed hard." Another decade passes, and it's the big day again. He gives the head monk a long stare and says, "I quit." "I'm not surprised," the head monk says, "You've been complaining ever since you got here."

Talking Dog. A guy spots a sign outside a house that reads, "Talking Dog for Sale." Intrigued, he walks in. "So what have you done with your life?" he asks the dog. "I've led a very full life," says the dog. "I lived in the Alps rescuing avalanche victims. Then I served my country in Iraq. And now I spend my days reading to the residents of a retirement home." The guy is flabbergasted. He asks the dog's owner, "Why on earth would you want to get rid of an incredible dog like that?" The owner says, "Because he's a liar! He never did any of that!"

Making Sure. Two hunters are out in the woods when one of them collapses. He's not breathing and his eyes are glazed. The other guy whips out his cell phone and calls 911. "I think my friend is dead!" he yells. "What can I do?" The operator says, "Calm down. First, let's make sure he's dead." There's silence, then a shot. Back on the phone, the guy says, "Okay, now what?"

Power of Perception. A turtle is crossing the road when he's mugged by two snails. When the police show up, they ask him what happened. The shaken turtle replies, "I don't know. It all happened so fast."

Tickle them

Tickling is really an art. It is a way to tease, get attention, and lovingly annoy your spouse. It can be the direct attack with limbs flailing or something sneakier like a feather on his neck. Whatever mode you prefer, it's a way to flirt and have some fun.

I think it's fun to jump my husband once he has gone to bed and tickle him into submission. Sometimes, I wait until he is almost asleep and then try to put his mustache hairs in his nose. I think this is hilariously funny (he does not).

He thinks it is more amusing to attack me while I am busy with something else, like bringing up a basket of laundry, cooking dinner, or talking on the phone with my mom. While very annoying, it is funny at the same time.

Regardless of your preferences, here are some ideas for tickling:

1. Set a playful mood. People who are not in a playful mood to begin with might be hard to tickle. Of course a little

tickling has been known to change a mood to playful very quickly. Joke around, have light conversation, and just get ready to have some fun.

2. Tickle the body with a feather. A feather is one of the best tickling tools known to man. The feather has the perfect amount of lightness and delicateness that makes our skin laugh with delight. Simply take a feather and lightly drag it across any part of the skin. The feather is for a light tickle that really just feels good and might get a few giggles in the process.

3. Tickle with your fingers. Lightly walk your fingers across the skin. Walk your fingers across the back of the shoulders, neck area, arms, feet, or legs. A light walking of the fingers will give a great tickling sensation.

4. Drag your fingernails across the skin. Lightly dragging your fingernails across your lover's skin will give a delightful tickle similar to that of the feather. Dragging your fingernails lightly across the skin can create a pleasant shivering sensation as well.

5. Give a little squeeze. Squeezing certain parts of the body is a great way to tickle. A little squeeze, or pinch, with your thumb and forefinger to the neck, buttocks, side, or knees can set off a delirious fit of laughter. Be careful not to squeeze so hard as to cause pain.

Hug them from behind when they are doing something

Surprise hugs are so nice, such as when you are cooking at the stove and your spouse comes up from behind and wraps his arms around you. Or when you are struggling over the computer, trying to get the pop-ups to stop their popping and you find yourself enveloped in a loving embrace.

The hugs from behind do not need to be quick embraces. Go ahead and stay awhile. Just hold your partner and rock gently back and forth as if you are slow dancing.

I don't know why we get stingy with hugs. They feel good and cost nothing. Yet too often we wait for a "reason" to hug instead of just doing it. Spontaneous hugs are exciting because they are just that—spontaneous.

Practice the art of hugging. Hug her when she is washing the car, vacuuming the house, or cleaning the kitchen. Hug him at the grocery store, on the golf course, and getting out of the shower. There doesn't have to be a reason. I guarantee that your spouse will like it.

Part V: Supporting and encouraging

Few things are more gratifying than living with your best friend. Marriage offers the perfect opportunity for such a life, especially if you create a climate of understanding and acceptance. Best friends listen to each other's problems, offer encouragement, and help each other laugh about problems. Spouses who are best friends keep secrets and confidences.

At our house, we call it "bedroom talk." This is not a conversation for the general public, or even our closest friends. This is our private talk that we know goes no further. We complain about our bosses, the president, and politicians in general. We discuss oil spills, education, health care legislation, and the mistakes that other parents seem to be making. We talk about golf, baseball, football, and the weather. And we laugh about little, daily events that demonstrate the craziness of life. In short, we are best friends.

And when one of us is struggling, we know where to turn. There is a ready ear that understands our perspective, our fears,

and our dreams. In the movie *Shall We Dance* starring Richard
Gere, Susan Sarandon, and Jennifer Lopez, Beverly Clark (Sarandon's character) explains the value of a long-term marriage this
way:

> Because we need a witness to our lives. There's a billion
> people on the planet, what does any one life really mean?
> But in a marriage, you're promising to care about every-
> thing. The good things, the bad things, the terrible things,
> the mundane things. All of it. All of the time. Every day.
> You are saying your life will not go unnoticed, because I
> will notice it. Your life will not go unwitnessed, because I
> will be your witness.

Your spouse is your witness. The one person who really sees
and understands what your life is all about. Here are some tips to
be your spouse's best friend.

Shut up and listen

We all like to talk, but few of us really know how to listen. Too often we act like we are "listening," yet really we are waiting for the opportunity to jump in with our own point of view. The whole time our spouse has been talking, we have been thinking about what we want to say, how we have the correct point of view, and why they are wrong. This is not the best way to communicate.

Nothing increases intimacy faster in a marriage than really listening to each other. This "meeting of the minds" happens when we really feel at least one other person on this earth really knows and cares about who we are.

Many couples do not understand that men and women communicate very differently. Men like to solve problems and women like to process information by talking. I have found this universally true with every couple I've ever been around. The woman starts to talk about something in her life, only to be interrupted by the husband with a "solution." She wasn't looking for the "solution," she only wanted to talk.

I can come home upset about my job and try to discuss this with my husband. His response? "Well, quit." Or I complain about a relative and my husband sums it up: "So don't see them anymore." This isn't what I am looking for. In fact, I am not looking for a solution at all. I just want to talk; maybe figure it out for myself.

This is one of the reasons that listening is so important. Too often, listening gets derailed by some of our behaviors. These include:

- Defensive body posture or tone. As soon as your partner starts to talk, you feel your defenses going up and become almost eager for the battle. You may cross your arms, look away, or use other gestures to push away what your partner is saying. As you brace yourself, your face shows an attitude that suggests to your spouse, "Go ahead . . . make my day!"
- Eye rolling. This technique makes it clear to your spouse that you do not value what he is saying. It is hardly worth your time! An obvious put-down, this behavior makes it clear you are not listening. It is impossible to have good eye contact or connection with your spouse if you are rolling your eyes.
- Head shaking. A technique intended to push away the words of your partner and communicate your disagreement even before her sentence is finished. Once you start shaking your head, usually you are no longer listening.
- Sighing. You are bored and you want to make sure everyone knows it. This technique did not work well for Vice President Al Gore in the 2000 presidential debates, and it will not work well for you. Your partner will resent it. Sigh-

ing indicates that you are not interested and can find a million other things more interesting to do. Stifle the sigh.

- Interrupting or cutting her off. Designed to "stop them cold," cutting the other off makes it clear you have only been waiting to "have your say" and are not interested in what she wishes to share. By interrupting, you make sure you get your chance to drive your point home but don't give your partner space to complete theirs.

Practice good listening skills by establishing eye contact, leaning forward, and nodding your head. Ask questions and use clarifying statements like, "Tell me about . . .," "Explain for me . . .," and "How do you feel about . . ." Show your partner you are really listening by repeating what you hear with phrases like, "So, I hear you say . . .," "I understand your position to be . . .," and "You seem to be concerned about . . ."

Talk at least five minutes each day together and really listen.

Buy them a pet

We are a cat family. We have always had cats; at least one, often two or three. Each time I tell my husband that I plan to bring one home, he emphatically says "no" and refuses to discuss the subject. When our daughter was three years old, he told her, "If you get another cat, I'm leaving." She promptly walked into the other room and brought out a small suitcase, handed it to her dad, and said, "We'll miss you, Daddy."

On the surface you would think my husband doesn't like the cats. Nothing could be further from the truth. This is just part of a game where he feigns total exasperation and annoyance each time we bring a new animal home. But under the surface is an affection and appreciation for animals in general and the two cats in particular that presently inhabit our house.

As soon as I bring home a new kitten, he goes crazy over it. He lies on the floor and plays with it, babies it, and teaches it to fetch. He trains the animals to come running as soon as he walks in the door. And, of course, the bed is full of cats at night.

Petting an animal can make us feel more relaxed, and there is research that shows there are health benefits of pet ownership. One recent study by researchers at the State University of New York, Buffalo, looked at the effects of pet ownership on 48 stock-brokers who were already taking medication for hypertension. It found that the 24 stockbrokers who were given a pet experienced a significant drop in high blood pressure compared with those without pets.[11]

The Web site for the Centers for Disease Control lists other benefits for pet owners, including a decrease in cholesterol and triglyceride levels, and decreased loneliness. Owning a pet can also increase your opportunities for exercise, outdoor activities, and socializing with other pet owners. The only caveat is that pets can sometimes prove to be highly toxic to people with allergies and asthma.

Pets just help make a family. Surprise your spouse with a new arrival.

Start a daily ritual

Rituals are the routines woven together that strengthen a marriage. Anything can become a ritual—you both just need to declare its existence. Many couples begin rituals after doing something together that is especially pleasant and fun. Announcing "We should do this every day, every week, or every year" is a great start.

There are many options for daily rituals:

- Have morning coffee together. Yes, it may not be possible to do this every day when one or both of you have to race off to work, but the times you can linger over a cup of coffee together can be very special. We like to go to the local cafe and sit outside sharing the newspaper. Of course, "having coffee" also means a running commentary on the news.
- Identify a favorite TV program (or two) to watch together. We have had favorite shows as long as I can remember. Years ago, it was *Thirty Something, ER,* and *Seinfeld.* Now

we love *Curb Your Enthusiasm* and *Justified*. Some couples like to watch "reality" TV and never miss the latest installment of *Survivor*. Whatever your taste, find a few programs that you both like and make it a ritual to watch them with a bowl of popcorn.

- Read in bed together. Many couples take advantage of this extra connection time by lying in bed and enjoying each other's company. Doing so can also lead to a spirited discussion about a book, article, or the latest news.
- Share a spiritual moment. In a University of Chicago survey, 75 percent of Americans who pray with their spouses reported that their marriages are "very happy" (compared with 57 percent of those who do not). Those who pray together are also more likely to say they respect each other and discuss their relationship together. Whether you have a simple grace at dinnertime or some soul-searching meditation, couples routinely say that a shared spiritual life helps keep them close.[12]
- Go for a walk. Walking together first thing in the morning or after dinner is a great way to get your exercise and connect. I find that we seem to walk a lot faster if we are stressed out or upset about something. But at the end of the walk, we both feel better and we have had a good dialogue.
- Call at lunchtime. A quick phone call to touch base is always a good idea. It provides an opportunity to share an amusing story about the day or simply vent on the latest memo from corporate. Happy couples make it a point to call each other—it's a nice break.

Build some rituals into your marriage and observe them regularly. These are the experiences that weave a close relationship.

Tape their favorite TV program

Most of us have favorite TV programs, series, or stars we like to watch. It is nice to find something you really want to watch when you sit down at the end of the day. Doing so use to sometimes be fairly difficult, but today many households have TiVo or another recording device as a part of their cable service that really simplifies "taping." You can now use the system to "tag" the shows you want to record and it will tape either one time or the whole series. With our system, we can also identify whether we want all episodes taped or just first-runs. It's great.

Need some ideas on what to tape? Here are some of the top shows that people record:

- *House.* This medical drama debuted in 2004 with the central character Dr. Gregory House. An unconventional medical genius, he often clashes with his boss, the hospital administrator Dr. Lisa Cuddy. Because his hypotheses about patients' illnesses are often based on subtle or controversial insights, the show is far-fetched but very popular. House's brusque, rude bedside manner and pill-popping habits leave you wondering what really goes on in health care.

- *The Simpsons.* This is now the longest-running American sitcom, the longest running animated program, and in 2009 surpassed *Gunsmoke* as the longest-running American primetime entertainment series. It is a satirical parody of a working-class American family as played by family members Homer, Marge, Bart, Lisa, and Maggie. The show is set in the fictional city of Springfield and lampoons American culture, society, and many aspects of the human condition.

- *Scrubs.* This show follows the lives of several employees of the fictional Sacred Heart teaching hospital. It features fast-paced, slapstick, and surreal vignettes, the latter presented as daydreams.

- *Seinfeld.* This series created by Larry David and Jerry Seinfeld features Seinfeld in a fictionalized version of himself. Set on Manhattan's Upper West Side, the show ran from 1989 to 1998 and features a host of Jerry's friends, including George Costanza, Elaine Benes, and Cosmo Kramer. Presently in syndication, *Seinfeld* remains popular, with a fan base that loves watching these four characters get themselves into bizarre predicaments.

- *The Twilight Zone.* I doubt if there is an episode my husband hasn't seen, but he still likes to tape this program. Created by Rod Serling, each of the 156 episodes in the original series is a mixture of fantasy, science fiction, and suspense. Many conclude with an unexpected twist at the end.

- *Lost.* This series aired from September 2004 to May 2010 and follows the lives of various groups and people who are survivors of a commercial passenger jet flying between Sydney and Los Angeles. The plane lands on a mysterious tropical island somewhere in the South Pacific.

- *I Love Lucy.* This old sitcom (1951–57), starring Lucille Ball, Desi Arnaz, Vivian Vance, and William Frawley was the most watched show in the United States in four of its six seasons. It remains in syndication across the world and its comedy is timeless. Some scenes, like Lucy trying to wrap chocolates moving along a conveyor belt, have become classics.

What are your spouse's favorite shows? Arrange to tape them so that you never miss an episode.

Ask them questions about things they are interested in

Yawn, I know. These may not be things that you are interested in. But so what? The thing just may be important to them. Now, I am fairly certain that my husband has very little interest in patterns for dining room curtains. But one day he sat still for a fairly long time, feigning interest as I described the options available.

I can assure you that I have absolutely no curiosity about the standardized testing that my husband conducts in the school system where he works, but I try to ask reasonably intelligent questions anyway. The point is, I show that I am interested.

Asking questions has even more importance if your spouse is really passionate about something. You darn well better learn something about the subject so that you can participate in a discussion of the details.

There are two types of questions you can use to glean information from your partner. They are very different in character and usage: closed questions and open questions. A closed question can be answered with either a single word or a short phrase. For example, "How old are you?" and "Where do you live?" are closed questions. Closed questions can often be answered with a simple "yes" or "no." Closed questions have the following characteristics:

- They give you facts.
- They are easy to answer.
- They are quick to answer.
- They keep control of the conversation with the questioner.

Open questions deliberately seek a longer and more comprehensive answer. They are structured to avoid a "yes" or "no" answer. Open questions have the following characteristics:

- They ask the respondent to think and reflect.
- They provide opinions and feelings.
- They hand control of the conversation to the respondent.

Open questions create the opportunity for a deeper level of communication. They make it clear that you are interested and available for listening. Open questions begin with words like "what," "why," "how," and "describe."

When opening conversations, a good balance includes around three closed questions to one open question. The closed questions help start the conversation and summarize progress, and the open question helps the other person to think and continue to provide useful information about the subject.

Demonstrate your interest by asking questions and showing interest in what is important to your spouse. You will find that both of your lives are richer when you share with each other.

Get along with their relatives (even if you don't)

Few things provide more humor than talking about families. It doesn't matter who you talk with, where they come from, or their socioeconomic status, most people have stories about their families. I am reminded of a cartoon that showed a support group meeting for an organization called "Adult Children from Normal Families." The room was empty.

All families have their interesting characters, and your partner's will be no exception. Although you may be fortunate and find some lifelong friends with your in-laws, you may also find a few people who are challenging to be around. What you have to remember is that they are still family and your spouse has feelings for them. As one husband explained to me, "I can cut down my family, but I don't want to hear it from anyone else." The old saying that "blood is thicker than water" is certainly true.

There is a lot of value in keeping the peace with your in-laws and out-laws. Yes, his mother is weird. Of course, her brother-in-law is a fascist, but do you have to keep mentioning it? Trust me, he already knows that his father drools while he eats. She is well aware that her aunt's artificial breasts look ridiculous. Everyone can see that grandpa's toupee has bald spots. Just make a point of it to be polite and laugh about it later.

Resist the temptation to get involved in family problems even if there are attempts to draw you in. I always ask myself the question, "Whose problem is it?" If it does not directly relate to me, I try to stay out of the middle. Remember, if you are in the middle when the arrows start to fly, you are the one who will get hit.

Make a point of it to be very polite and gracious when your spouse's relatives are about. Even if you don't particularly care for them, you can certainly be welcoming a couple of times a year. Make polite conversation, and avoid debates over anything more critical than flower arrangements. Stay out of the gossip and refuse to play "ain't it awful" with the family complainer. Ignore the comparisons and critical comments that are meant to be "helpful." Just present yourself and your home as a page out of Miss Manners.

I remember one time complaining to my mother about my mother-in-law, and she interrupted me, saying, "Well, she did one thing right."

"What's that?" I asked.

"She raised a nice man for you to marry."

Good point.

Compliment them in public

It's great to say nice things to your spouse, but even better in front of other people. Let other people know how highly you think of your spouse by bragging about his achievements, her latest projects, or something nice he has done. Rather than taking credit for the new purchase, great dinner, or children's good grades, let your spouse know how much you appreciate their efforts by mentioning it in public.

Never underestimate the value of a compliment. Given sincerely and openly, it shows your appreciation and caring. The main guideline to giving a compliment is to be sincere and genuine. Ask yourself to recognize what is important, what needs to be spoken, and what can be offered as a selfless gift.

Use "I" messages to convey your compliments. For example, rather than saying, "You are such a funny joke teller," you can say, "I love the way you tell jokes and make me laugh." A good "I" message is more easily accepted. In addition, "I" messages are personal revelations, while "you" messages are judgments.

Some examples of sentences that reflect "I" statements are:

One thing I value about you . . .
One thing I admire about you . . .
I think it was really inspiring the way you . . .

It may feel a bit awkward to give or receive compliments if you are not used to doing so. But it can also help you to start noticing good things about yourself and your spouse, increase positive energy, and bring a sense of connection. A sincere compliment, whether given or received, can transform the day and make you feel like a good person. What could be bad about that?

Accept compliments

Now that we have the compliments flying, let's not push them away. Often we find it difficult to take in positive messages and compliments. We grow nervous or defensively brush off the kind words that our spouse says about us. Sometimes, we may even discount flattering remarks and begin to argue with the compliment giver. I see this all the time. Your wife mentions how nice your hair looks and you point out that you really need a haircut. Or your husband mentions the nice skirt you are wearing and you explain how old it is.

Reasons we may reject compliments include:

- Analyzing the compliment and wondering, "What did they really mean?"
- Feeling unworthy or undeserving of the compliment.
- Expecting the compliment to be followed with a criticism.
- Rejecting compliments due to insecurity or poor self-esteem.

- Simply not knowing how to handle the compliment.

What's important about receiving compliments is that it opens your heart to yourself. You can begin to see yourself through another person's eyes. You can notice yourself in a new light, and become aware of what is right about you. You can acknowledge that you are good and worthy, lovable and likable. Compliments allow you to know and accept yourself. You can love yourself today and love yourself for who you will become tomorrow.

One of the most simple, effective, and graceful ways to accept a compliment is to say a simple "Thank you." You do not need to offer rebuttals, return compliments, or provide explanations. Here are a few effective, sample responses to a compliment:

- Thank you. I appreciate that.
- Thank you, your words mean a lot to me.
- Thank you, I value your input.
- Thank you, that is very kind.
- Thank you. I had a lot of help reaching for this success.

Try out a few of these responses until you find one that you feel comfortable saying. The next time your spouse compliments you, throw your arms around them and say it in their ear.

Say "please" and "thank you"

There is a rule of thumb that I use when I counsel young couples. I tell them, "Treat each other at least as nice as you would treat a total stranger." They usually giggle when I say that, absolutely convinced that of course this is already true at their house.

But in many households, including mine at times, this is not true at all. We take out all our daily frustrations and problems on the person closest to us. We forget the common courtesies that we would extend to someone standing in the check-out line at Target. We forget to say "please" and "thank you."

You wouldn't scream at the person ahead of you in line that he is taking too long and acting stupid. You wouldn't grab your purchase out of the clerk's hand to let her know that you are frustrated with waiting. No, most of us maintain politeness, even if we are exasperated with the whole ordeal.

At home, however, some of us check our best behavior at the door. We fail to remember even the basics of a "please" and "thank you." We walk into the house as if we have a right to puke our bad day on anyone in our way. Sometimes, we assume that courtesies are not even necessary. After all, isn't taking out the garbage his job? Doesn't she always do the laundry? How pleasant it would be to hear an occasional "thank you."

Common courtesy is the oil that greases a marriage. In our fast-paced lives, a little extra grease is especially important.

Forget mistakes

Yes, I said, forget the mistakes. Let them go. Get over them. Sometimes referred to as "museum pieces," mistakes are the fodder for arguments and resentment. I know, there are some mistakes, like infidelity, you just can't forget. Well, then, give marriage counseling some serious thought so that you have every chance to start anew.

Most mistakes in marriage, though, are little annoying things like not paying a bill, backing the new car into a light pole, or leaving one of the neighbor kids at Chuck E. Cheese. Well, maybe these things aren't so little, after all. Speaking as one who frequently backs into solid objects with the car, I assure you, this can be annoying to one's spouse. My husband always asks me the same question: "Didn't you see it?" Seems like a dumb inquiry to me. Of course I didn't see it—I wouldn't have hit it had I seen it. And let's be clear. It was he who left a kid at Chuck E. Cheese's after our daughter's birthday party one year!

What I see in happy marriages is that spouses not only work

at letting go of their partner's mistakes, they eventually laugh about them and simply accept these things with some humor. We all do things in the course of our lives that weren't the best decision, could have been done better, or were simply "brainless." You know, that state of being where you just weren't thinking at all.

Nothing is worse than having an instant replay of everything you have done wrong each time you disagree with your spouse. Who wants to wallow through all this debris all over again? Let go of mistakes and agree that you won't bring up the museum pieces when you are angry.

Hanging on to mistakes can build resentment, an emotionally debilitating condition that interferes with good relationships. It can have a variety of negative results on the person experiencing it, including touchiness or edginess, denial of anger or other emotions, and easy provocation or anger toward the other person. It can also lead to more long-term effects, such as a hostile, cynical, or sarcastic attitude that may become a barrier in the relationship. Resentment produces a lack of personal and emotional growth, difficulty in self-disclosure and trusting others, and loss of self-confidence.

Let go of mistakes and don't bring up the past. At our house, we are not allowed to bring up anything from the past unless it is pleasant. If this is difficult for the two of you, get a jar and label it "museum pieces." Anytime one of you brings up a past mistake, put $5 in the jar. When the jar is full, go out to dinner together. This will help eliminate the practice.

Reserve a hotel room when you visit the in-laws

Family is great, especially with a little space. Even if you get along fine with your in-laws, both you and your spouse will find a visit less stressful if you stay at a hotel. Yes, I know, the in-laws will insist that you be their guests. Initially, they may even insist with pouting lips that you "simply must stay" with them. But guests, like fish, quickly begin to reek. And really, who wants to know all the little habits and quirks of a household full of adults? A little distance makes for harmonious relationships.

If you have children and your in-laws are still insisting on being the host, dump the kids and take a well-deserved break. This can turn out great for all involved—becoming special bonding time between the grandchildren and their grandparents and private time for the two of you. Or the in-laws may find out why some species eat their young and decide that you were right after all: staying all together at their house is a bad idea.

Regardless, staying at a hotel is so much more fun. It allows you the flexibility to be on your schedule, not someone else's. You can get up when you want, eat when you want, and not walk out of the bathroom after a shower, draped in a towel too short and into a room too full of glaring relatives. If you are traveling without children, it can be a wonderful break from your routine and create some special moments.

We recently stayed at the Stanley Hotel in Estes Park, Colorado. This beautiful, historic hotel was the inspiration for Stephen King's book *The Shining*. Our room was on the 4th floor (known for paranormal activity) and had a slanting roof, pillow-top bed, and large-screen TV. In the morning, we got our coffee and went back to bed. As we sipped our lattes, we watched *The Shining* on TV; it plays continuously at the Stanley.

It was a moment made in heaven. When do people on the go ever get the chance to do something like this? Most of the time, we hit the ground running as soon as the alarm sounds. Coffee is sipped on the run, not as a leisurely event on a pillow-top bed. And there is certainly no opportunity for some fun snuggling.

Look for opportunities for fun when you visit the in-laws. Some families have "destination" reunions where they meet in Hawaii, Florida, or on a cruise ship. These are great ways to connect but still afford the opportunity for everyone to have some space and individual fun.

Give heavy doses of encouragement

Encouragement is very different from praise. Praise is given for a job well done, completed, finished. The problem with praise is that often the people who need it the least get it the most. We all remember the know-it-all kid who was always raising his hand in grade school. That brown-noser always got the most attention, the best assignments, and early recess for his efforts. But what about the kid in the back who was really struggling? This is the one who really could have benefited from a little attention. Some encouragement for him might have made a difference.

Encouragement, in contrast, is given for any effort, any improvement. Like milestones on the road to success, it marks progress and propels people to try harder.

I remember writing my first book. There were not a lot of people who offered much encouragement. The usual response when I explained what I was doing was more like, "Right. And who is going to publish it?" Few friends asked about progress on the manuscript. No one requested an opportunity to read an excerpt. And no one came forward to claim an early copy for review.

The only people in my life who really backed me were my mother and my husband. My mother offered money, resources, and encouragement to keep the project on course. She called daily, insisting that there is no such thing as "writer's block," that a writer just has to keep typing.

My husband was the other cheerleader. I remember one particular low point in the effort where I was really struggling. I desperately felt that I needed an advisor to help me with the structure and chapter titles, but I had very little money—a common dilemma for writers.

My husband walked into my office after cashing his paycheck and started laying $100 bills on my desk. He said, "Hire the help you need." I was amazed. After all, I had never written a book, never been published, or even attempted writing before. He just made it clear that he believed in me and would help me make it happen.

That is encouragement.

Do one of your spouse's chores

One of the advantages of marriage is that you can create a division of labor by sharing the chores. You wash the clothes—he folds them. He buys the groceries—you cook them. You pay the bills—he does the taxes. There are many different kinds of arrangements, but most long-term marriages fall into a pattern of sharing the work.

I found out how ingrained this pattern is when my husband had hernia surgery. Naturally, he was told that he shouldn't do any lifting, so I immediately took over his chores, including taking out the garbage. He came home from work and saw what I had done. Getting all excited, he just kept mentioning how wonderful this was, and how great I was.

I started to laugh. I do dozens of chores around the house including paying all the bills, cleaning our home, doing the laundry, and so forth. But all of a sudden to do one of "his" chores is a big deal. That's exactly the point. It is not expected and therefore is a surprise.

Doing repetitive and boring chores is tiresome for most of us. That's why folks don't like to do them. And some people still think women are doing more than their share. According to an MSNBC survey, respondents were asked if "the chores in their household were performed by just one person or if they were shared." The men responded differently from the women. Seventy-four percent of male respondents said the chores were shared, but only 51 percent of the women agreed.

Chores are a leading source of conflict in marriages. If you ask wives what one of their top stressors is, quite a few will respond that it is the fact that their husbands don't want to do their share of work around the house. Stress levels increase in your home when either one of you is unhappy about unfinished chores.

Couples fight over who does what around the house almost as much as they fight over money. According to the 2000 U.S. Census, even though many women work outside the home, they still tend to do most of the household chores.

Marriage is, in many ways, a business partnership. The business is running the house. That means keeping financial records, maintenance, shopping, planning, cleaning, cooking, child care, transportation, and so on. When the business runs smoothly, there is more peace and harmony.

George Eliot wrote, "What do we live for, if it is not to make life less difficult for each other?" What can you do to make your partner's life less difficult?

Leave them notes

Notes are great. They are easy to give and very fun to get. This is a surefire, inexpensive way to improve your marriage. They can be as simple as a sticky note or more complicated with computer graphics. Whatever the format, they give a lift to anyone's day.

You can leave notes in expected places—on the counter, the dresser, or pillow. Or consider putting them in a surprising location, like the shower. You can put them in the car, in a notebook, or stuffed in a suitcase. What makes notes so special is that they are unexpected. You open your briefcase and there is an "I love you" clinging to the inside. You open your sock drawer and there is a picture with a message just for you.

The content of the notes does not really matter. They can be very short and sweet. They are especially effective if they reference a private joke or a recent incident that only the two of you know about. This is the opportunity for pet names, inside jokes, and special intimacies that just the two of you understand.

My husband went on a note craze several years ago. He made cards on the computer that reflected his love of football. Pictures of a quarterback, football field, and goalposts were highlighted with comments like, "Go for the touchdown of love!" or "You are my quarterback in the game of love." I loved those homemade cards. I still have them in my treasure drawer.

I like to purchase note cards whenever I find some that are unusual. They are available in most gift stores, drugstores, and large supermarkets. I prefer the ones with a bit of humor and then I add a personal note.

Surprise your partner with a note from time to time. It is sure to brighten her day.

Plan a "good news" celebration

I don't think we celebrate enough. Sure, we all celebrate weddings, anniversaries, and birthdays, but that leaves a lot of other days that could use a boost. I think it is really fun to celebrate some of the smaller things that happen in our lives: a new job, our best golf game, or just a beautiful day.

Celebrations don't need to be complicated; a nice dinner with a bottle of wine will do. I still remember when we first got married and money was very tight. I went out and bought an expensive steak for dinner and planned a special meal. Feeling guilty about the money, I called my mother, who said, "Sometimes when you can afford it the least is when you need it the most." Good point.

Most of us don't take enough opportunity to celebrate the good news in our lives. Celebrate Fridays, the first sweet corn of the season, or a bonus in the paycheck. Rejoice over a promotion, a new job, or getting rid of the old boss. Party hardy when relatives visit and especially when they leave. And commemorate special events that the two of you enjoy, like the first day of spring.

Look for opportunities to find a "good news" reason to celebrate in your marriage. It's fun and your partner will appreciate it.

Listen to their dreams

Somewhere along the road of living we stop, dismiss, or deny our dreams. We all had lots of dreams as kids—going to the moon, becoming a superhero, competing in the Olympics, or just riding a two-wheeler. But dreaming doesn't need to stop when you grow up. There are lots of new dreams that you can have, and it's even better when someone wants to listen to them.

You can listen to your spouse's dreams and help them imagine. She may have dreams of a new career, a special vacation, or just improving her skill as an oil painting hobbyist. He may talk about what he "always" wanted to do or something he wants to change. Regardless, this is a great time to turn out the light, snuggle under the covers, and talk.

Although many couples just "expect" to stay together, dedicated couples share a vision of the future and want to stay together. Sharing dreams makes reaching that future together more likely. Here are some steps to nurture your vision of the future together:

- Set goals. You cannot walk in the same direction until you both agree on the destination. Goals are planned steps along the way that make your dreams a reality. Set specific, realistic, short-term, and long-term goals for your finances, your children, and fun things that will enhance your relationship and bring you closer together. Since you both know your joint expectations, setting goals helps reduce the chance of conflict.
- Continue to share your dreams. Dreams involve our deepest hopes. Though difficult at first, the more committed you tend to be, and the more committed you are, the easier it is to share. Sharing dreams allows you to understand the "deeper regions" of each other and makes it easier to move dreams into the category of goals.
- Plan future fun. It's fun to plan for fun, whether it's a special date next week or a getaway weekend in several months. This is a dream turned into action, and you will both have something to look forward to—together.
- Consider making a "bucket list" together. These are the things you absolutely want to do before you "kick the bucket." This idea has gained popularity since the movie of the same name featuring Jack Nicholson and Morgan Freeman. Here are some of the activities on our bucket list, some of which we have already accomplished:

1. *Visit as many of the continents as possible.* We have no interest in going to Antarctica, but the others—South America, Africa, Asia, Australia, and Europe—have great appeal. The leading cities in Europe all are a wealth of history and culture and the people are fascinating. Consider a river tour through Italy or a cruise on the Mediterranean.
2. *Bike through Europe.* This takes a bit of planning, but it beats taking in the country through a passenger-side

window. Many areas have paved bike paths and you can use the Eurail train system to get from one country to another.

3. *Ride an elephant.* Yes, we've done the rides at the zoo, but it would be a lot of fun to do this on a nature preserve in Africa. Sitting two stories high to see the scenery would be a unique experience.

4. *Take a fishing expedition to Canada.* There are thousands of beautiful lakes that you can fly in to with a guide. They provide all the equipment, know the best fishing spots, and arrange lodging. Hopefully, they will also take the fish off the hook.

5. *Raft down the Colorado River.* There are numerous expedition groups that can arrange everything and make this trip a real memory maker. Go for at least a week and sign up with one of the tour services that arrange the food, lodging, and all the details. Then sit back, enjoy the scenery, and sleep under the stars.

6. *Visit a "real" blues bar in Chicago.* If you are looking for the soul of the blues, look no further. Chicago has many great blues venues, including Buddy Guy's Legends, Kingston Mines, Chicago Blues, and Blues R & B. Spend a night in the Windy City and take the architectural river tour the next day.

7. *Skydive.* The trend now is to do tandem jumps where you hook up to a jumpmaster and he handles all the details, like pulling the rip cord. This is a great way to skydive if you don't want to spend a lot of time learning how. Doing the dive solo, however, is even more of a thrill. Many clubs have a "ground school" where they teach you to dive solo. There are few things as exhilarating as plummeting toward the ground at seventy miles an hour.

8. *Ski the Alps.* Many of us have skied in Colorado, Utah, and Idaho, but what about Europe? France, Austria, Italy, and Switzerland all have ski resorts with beautiful scenery, great restaurants, and local flavor.

9. *Go heli-skiing.* The access to snow and terrain by way of helicopter is different (and better) than anything else you can experience as a skier. Offered at most major ski resorts, it is pricey but well worth the money. You need to be an intermediate, advanced, or expert skier to try this one.

10. *Swim with the dolphins.* You can find places to do this in Florida and the Bahamas. There are some who feel that this activity has magical healing powers, but I think it is just fun. Dolphins are very friendly creatures and seem to like the attention.

11. *Learn to surf.* This will entertain you all day as you learn how to balance and ride the waves. Most beaches have places where you can rent a surfboard. Hawaii has some of the best surfing in the world, and the water is warm.

12. *Scuba dive or snorkel the Great Barrier Reef in Australia.* This is the largest coral reef in the world and has the most unique aquatic environment. You can stay right on the beach and have access to the reef offshore or take an excursion by boat to some of the islands. You will see an enchanting array of aquatic life.

13. *Go to Israel.* If you like history, artifacts, and museums, this is the place to go. As one tour guide said, "You can stay for six weeks, six months, or six years. You will never see everything." Our brief two-week stay left us wanting more. By the way, it is very safe. The people love American money.

14. *Climb an active volcano, preferably when it is not erupting.* Mount Vesuvius, located on the Bay of Naples, Italy,

is an excellent choice for this activity. It is the only volcano on the European mainland to have erupted within
the last hundred years. It is best known for its eruption
in a.d. 79, which led to the destruction of the Roman cities of Pompeii and Herculaneum and the death of their
inhabitants. When you go, take a side trip to Pompeii
and tour the remains of this ancient city.

15. *Swim in the Dead Sea.* Full of minerals, the sea enables
you to float effortlessly, owing to the density of the water. It is a unique experience. The water is so "thick" that
boats cannot float on the water; they just flip over.

16. *Attend the Olympics.* Whatever needs saying about the
commercialism of the Olympic Games, they are one of
the biggest and most exciting events on the planet. Find
the time and location that can work for you and treat
yourself to this unique experience.

17. *Spend a month in Paris.* Referred to as the "City of Love,"
it is a magical place of museums, cafes, restaurants, and
attractions. Don't miss Moulin Rouge with the minia-
ture horses, juggling, and can-can dancing.

18. *Walk the Great Wall of China.* Dubbed one of the Seven
Wonders of the Medieval World, the Great Wall winds
up and down across deserts, grasslands, mountains,
and plateaus across China. It spans approximately 5,500
miles from east to west. With a history of more than
2,000 years, it is a unique attraction, owing to its architectural grandeur and historical significance.

19. *Attend a Super Bowl.* This is the premier championship
game between the National Football League and the
American Football League. The location changes every
year and tickets are pricey, but this is a must-attend for
any football fan.

20. *Tour Alaska.* Take a cruise or a series of land excursions
to see this beautiful state. Don't miss Denali National

Park, which features North America's tallest mountain, Mount McKinley, at 20,320 feet. The park also features a complete subarctic ecosystem with large mammals such as grizzly bears, wolves, Dall sheep, and moose.

Some of the happiest times you can have as a couple are when you share your dreams. You may find that you have some dreams in common, and those dreams can turn into plans. Dreaming and planning together for the future gives you a focus and a goal. You can then sit back and enjoy the journey.

Ban "always" and "never" from your vocabulary

These are fighting words. The first reaction anyone has when he hears them is to throw up his defenses. When your spouse says, "You never do that," or "You are always that way," your first response is to disagree. After all, sometimes you *have* done the thing identified. And no, you are not *always* "that way."

These wild generalizations only muddy the water of any good argument, with everyone getting defensive. And the more defensive you both get, the less likely you will be able to resolve the conflict. Nothing shuts down communication faster than "always" and "never."

Consider "always" statements. When you say to your spouse you "always" do this or that, what you are intending to say is that your spouse did not do something that you expected her to do. The problem with this is that you are expecting your spouse to correctly interpret the message that is usually hidden in the sentence. I say "hidden" because odds are your spouse can't read your mind and will miss what you're saying.

For example, this past week you took out the trash and put it in the garbage can. Unfortunately, you forgot to put a new trash bag in the kitchen container. Your spouse noticed and said, "You always forget to put a new bag in the trash container." You now come to the (incorrect) conclusion that your spouse is only trying to goad you by grossly exaggerating. The result? You dismiss not only your spouse's statement, but also your spouse. Your spouse only wanted you to remember to put a trash bag in the container, but that's not what you heard. What you heard was, "You bird-brain. Even a trained seal could remember a task this simple!" This is why "always" statements slam the door on communications. They are demeaning to the person at the receiving end.

Now let's talk about the "never" statement. This is very similar to the "always" statement and has the same effect of shutting down communication. One of the most common "never" sentences that spouses hear is "You never listen to me." People shut their ears as soon as they hear these words. It is their cue that the conversation is over, because "never" is an exaggeration (or simply not the truth).

There are two things that you can do for each other. First, don't use sentences that include "always" or "never." Those sentences have the opposite effect from what you want to achieve. As a general rule, men and women tend not to be great communicators with each other. Using sentences with "always" and "never" only makes this proclivity worse.

We used to charge each other $1 whenever one of us used these words. This extinguished the bad habit very quickly.

Say, "I have confidence in you," and say it often

What beautiful words to hear: "I have confidence in you." This is not something most of us hear routinely in our daily walks of life. Having one person in your life who lets you know he has faith in you is invaluable. Trust me; there are more people who would like to see you fail than see you succeed.

I learned this lesson a long time ago when I had the opportunity to appear as a guest on *The Phil Donahue Show.* His "people" called the agency where I worked because we had developed a program for nurses with an addiction to drugs. After booking us for the show, they made all the arrangements for a limo to pick us up, do our makeup and hair, and brief us for the appearance. Filmed in front of a studio audience, the show was broadcast to millions of people. And there I sat onstage as one of the experts.

The shock hit me when I returned to work. No one congratulated me or let me know that I had done a good job. On the contrary, most of my co-workers barely said "Hi." And when lunchtime came, I was not included in the lunch group. As one outspoken employee said, "Why did you get to be on the show? You don't have as much experience in counseling as I do. They should have picked someone with more experience." That may have been true, but they had picked me.

This is why the home roost is so important. It is the one place, the one relationship, that is always on your side. And when you struggle with a new challenge, your spouse may be the one person who can let you know that you can succeed.

Text them during the day with little messages

Personally, I'm not entirely sold on texting. Several years ago, however, my kids told me that they really preferred that I would text them rather than leave a voice mail. What? How could they not want to hear my voice? My daughter gently pointed out that all my voice mails sound pretty much the same, and she didn't have time to listen. Good point.

Texting gives immediate access to someone else, with, often, an immediate response. You can "reach out and touch someone" without its taking a lot of time. It works well when your spouse really can't answer the phone or is too busy, but you just want to touch base. I have learned to use it as a regular way to connect with my husband during the day.

It's helpful to learn a few of the standard abbreviations. Here are some of the most popular:

gtg   got to go
lol   laughing out loud

rofl	rolling on the floor laughing
btw	by the way
sup	what's up
fyi	for your information
asap	as soon as possible
w/	with
BF	boyfriend
b4	before
cos	because
GF	girlfriend
jk	just kidding
l8r	later
thx	thanks
xoxo	hugs and kisses
zzzz	sleeping or bored
cya	see ya

By committing these to memory, you can surprise your spouse and family with your texting expertise.

Take a yoga class

Why, you may ask, should you take a yoga class to improve your marriage? Because it will relax you and help you to "let go." This was suggested by a friend of mine who was struggling with issues with her husband. She discovered that she was actually making things worse by nagging, cajoling, correcting, and yelling at him to force him to change.

She discovered that she was a part of the problem. As long as she persisted in her behavior, he also continued his. After beginning yoga, she became much calmer and clearer. She could now put into perspective problems that had seemed overwhelming. She used the yoga to let go and focus on her own shortcomings instead of those of her husband.

Her experience is typical of those who practice yoga. Though known as a set of physical practices that include gentle stretches, breathing exercises, and progressive deep relaxation, the original goal of yoga is to prepare the body and mind for meditation.

These meditative practices also follow a sequence. First developed is the capacity to withdraw the senses from focus on the outer world, then, the capacity to concentrate on a meditative subject—a candle flame, an image, or the movement of the breath. Finally, and for most only occasionally, this concentration leads to a wordless and timeless experience of inner peace.

Finding peace and serenity can dramatically improve your marriage. People who worry a lot and hold on to problems find themselves anxious and frustrated. Here are some tips to let go of problems in your life:

- Make a list of the things in your past that have made you angry and still cause you pain. Reflect on the list and realize that those things are unlikely to happen again.
- Change the way you think about others' actions. Recognize that there were reasons they made the choices they did even if you don't understand or even know what those reasons were.
- Recognize that the only person who makes no mistakes is the person who does nothing. Forgive the mistakes of others and refuse to let regret rob you of happiness.
- Make a conscious commitment to release others' power over your life. Remember, the only person that you can change is yourself.
- Understand that it's okay to love someone even if they aren't perfect.

Take the time every day to just enjoy "quiet" so that you can listen to your soul. You may be surprised at the messages you receive.

Apologize, even if you did nothing wrong

A lot of people don't understand the art of apologizing. They think that saying "I'm sorry" requires doing something terribly wrong. You do not need to commit an unpardonable sin to apologize; apologies can be used for everyday misunderstandings or hurt feelings.

You can apologize without admitting any fault or intent on your part. You can apologize that your spouse feels so sad, or is so angry, or you disappointed her in some way. After all, you probably are sorry. You don't want the brouhaha that is occurring at your house. You would like things to settle down.

There are times, though, when we make mistakes—serious mistakes, mistakes that hurt our partner and our relationship. Here are some "do's" for giving a sincere apology:

- Take the time to reflect on what you did wrong—and then take a little more time to reflect on what you did wrong.
- Use words that are very clear and that accurately convey

your thoughts and sentiments. Be honest and show true sincerity when apologizing.

- Use words that convey that you understand the other person's hurt feelings, and can appreciate why they are angry. Trying to convey or justify your feelings will likely be interpreted as your missing the point of an apology.
- When it comes to selecting from among the many approaches to apologizing, be sure to select the one that plays to your strengths. A letter is a much better option if you happen to be a very nervous person, or find face-to-face very difficult. If you go this route, be sure to take the time to craft the written apology carefully and run through a few re-reads to make sure the phrasing is perfect. Put it down and revisit the letter the next day for the final draft before giving it to your partner.
- Be as specific as you can about the mistake, and as clear as you can about your responsibility. Make sure the apology clearly conveys that you recognize not only why but how much your partner was injured by your actions. Saying "I know you were hurt" is not the same as saying "I know how incredibly insulted and angry you were because of . . ." The latter is a much better way to convey that you're accepting responsibility.
- Allow your spouse the time to think about your apology— the time they take may vary but the offended person has the right to determine how much time that should be.
- Clearly request forgiveness but don't expect or demand it.
- Be prepared to accept that your spouse might not forgive you, and acknowledge to them that you are prepared for that possibility and will accept it.
- Give some thought (and then some more thought) to when and how you should apologize.

- Say "I'm sorry I was rude," not "I'm sorry if I was rude." "If" is one of those potentially costly qualifiers that can turn a good apology into a really bad one, so be careful. Words really matter. "I apologize for insulting you" is much better than "I apologize if what I said seemed insulting or offensive." And "I'm sorry I hurt your feelings" is never as strong as "I'm sorry I called you an idiot."
- Make it genuine and never justify your actions.

Here are some "don'ts" for apologizing:

- Don't try to evoke sympathy for yourself as part of the apology.
- Never assume the issue is minor. Err on the side of accepting the importance and seriousness of the mistake. Assuming this is a big deal to the other person when in fact it really isn't, is a much better place to be in than the alternative.
- When preparing a verbal apology, be sure to avoid anything that could mistakenly be interpreted as insincerity— bad jokes, rolling your eyes, avoiding eye contact, excessive shuffling, or nervous twitching.
- Avoid apologizing for the wrong mistake, just because that mistake is easier to fix or forgive.
- Don't simply describe or explain the offense and assume that this will suffice—it doesn't constitute an apology and will likely make things worse by insulting the other person's intelligence.
- Don't demand a response to your apology—be patient and wait.
- Don't constantly ask the other person why he is mad— assume there is a reason. If he is forced to clarify why he is hurt then you obviously don't get it.

- If you give an apology, don't use it as an opportunity to offer a few excuses.
- Avoid all qualifiers and hidden messages that might imply sharing responsibility for the problem or mistake—never share the blame.
- Never use the word "but" when giving an apology.

Practice sincere apologizing in your marriage. It will help you both to accept and love each other even though you are not perfect.

Accept apologies

Now that you have learned to give apologies, it is equally important for you to know how to accept them. Too often I have couples come to therapy because they harbor years of anger and resentment over injuries that have occurred. Like bricklayers, they have added bitterness to their memory one brick at a time until they have a wall which separates them from one another and effectively divides the relationship. Even if apologies have been issued, the recipient has not forgiven the transgression and it continues to fester.

Saying "I'm sorry" is one of the most difficult things for a person to do. It is a reaching out, a connection to rebuild a bridge that was damaged or destroyed. It is important to learn how to accept an apology, how to determine whether or not you should accept an apology, and what accepting it really means.

If your spouse has done something that has harmed you in some way, whether emotionally, physically, or monetarily, that doesn't necessarily mean they will feel the need to apologize. But if they do, and they would like to make amends, you now have to decide several things:

Do you want to accept the apology?
Can your spouse make amends?
Will you be able to extend trust back again?

Let's look first at the decision to accept the apology. If you are not able to truly forgive your spouse, then it becomes very difficult to accept the apology. Accepting is the same as agreeing that you understand why they wronged you and that they are going to attempt not to wrong you again. If you don't truly understand and are not willing to accept your partner's apology, then it's not right to offer a flippant "that's okay" response.

The second part of accepting an apology is deciding whether or not your spouse can, and is willing to, make amends. For small offenses, a simple assurance that the behavior will not be repeated is enough to make amends and accept the apology. But for larger issues, before you can truly accept the apology, you may need to consider whether your spouse can make and is willing to make amends, to somehow make restitution for the wrong done.

The third step in accepting an apology is asking the question, "Can I trust that the same mistake won't happen again?" Until you are able to extend trust to your partner again, you should not accept the apology. This ties into the next question to ask yourself: Do you really want to reconcile at this time? It's okay to hold off on accepting an apology until your spouse has made amends and you are ready to trust him again—in fact, it's better if you do not accept the apology until this is done.

Once you accept your spouse's apology for the wrongdoing and forgive her, then you can move on with your lives. Forgiveness isn't something you extend to the other person, but rather something you do inside yourself, for yourself. Accepting the other person's apology is something you can extend to the other person, but the real healing takes place within you.

The best way to accept an apology is to simply let your spouse know, clearly, that though what they did harmed you in some way, you choose to believe they will not harm you again. If your partner cannot express the reason for the apology, then the behavior is likely to continue.

Only you can decide if the wrong done to you that damaged your relationship can be repaired. If it's true that saying "I'm sorry" is one of the most difficult things to do, you should give that apology the same amount sincere consideration when choosing whether or not to accept it as the other person has in choosing to offer it.

Display their diplomas and awards

Receiving my high school diploma didn't mean much to me. I'm not saying it was not an important accomplishment, because it was, but I just always knew I would do it. But attending nursing school was totally different. This was something I wasn't sure I could do—even when I was well into it. One of my proudest days was when I graduated from this school after studying for three years. I took that diploma to a custom framer as soon as I received it and then hung it on my wall. It's been there ever since.

It was much the same thing when my husband received his college diploma. He was an "elderly" student, beginning his degree in his late thirties. He frequently said, "I just never thought I would go to college." When he graduated, he had his picture taken in a cap and gown and hung it next to his diploma on the wall.

We have always had a "trophy wall" at our house. We display awards, kind letters, certificates, and stars. And why not? These are things to be proud of.

Let your partner know how proud you are. Make sure you

display accomplishments and successes for all to see. They also serve as a reminder of success when you hit the inevitable speed bumps in life.

Tell them "I agree"

Just as simple as that: "I agree." No question, no argument, just an affirmation of your partner's position. Agreements are good—and it helps improve a marriage when you can find more areas of agreement than disagreement. But what if you don't agree? Then sometimes you just have to agree to disagree.

When it comes to marriage and problems, sometimes couples become too focused on winning an argument. The problem is that when you focus on winning, you are both deciding one of you has to be the loser. And no one likes to lose. Losing builds resentment and may mean future conflict is even more intense because winning has become so important.

Arguments usually erupt because the parties involved have different viewpoints. Your perspective and your spouse's perspective are different. But often there are conflicting ways to look at an issue and they both can be correct. "Truth" is flexible. What we observe is colored by our experiences and frame of reference.

This is why arguments with your spouse can be so irritating.

Both of you may feel slighted because you are convinced of the rightness of your "truth." When you accept that what you view as truth and what your spouse views as truth may be two entirely different things, you are a step closer to resolving your differences.

Instead of exasperation, try explanation and understanding. Instead of win-lose scenarios, ignore who is right and who is wrong. Accept what your partner is saying, and when possible, say "I agree."

Too many couples have the mistaken belief that they must work out every discussion, every disagreement, and every small contention that comes their way. They expend a great deal of energy arguing over the best laundry detergent, the most efficient way to pack the car, the optimal setting for the thermostat, the importance of making the bed with decorative throw pillows, and the personality characteristics of certain relatives. They may explore, at length, the correctness of each other's personal habits—the importance of flossing, the best toothpaste, and the classic debate: which way the toilet paper should hang, over or under. "Over," of course, is the correct answer (just kidding).

I have witnessed discussions in which each partner insists on the rightness of his position with remarkable vigor and repetition. The debaters may produce receipts, documents, and spreadsheets to support their positions. Random calls may be made to innocent bystanders with requests at short notice to confirm a particular point of view. A quick check of the Internet may be used to locate research studies or other statistical material that proves, once and for all, the validity of a particular opinion.

A point is reached somewhere between the thirty-seventh and fiftieth discussion of the same issue, when husband and wife may as well agree that they will never agree. After all, both members of the union have already eagerly promoted their respective points of view comprehensively and convincingly.

Although it may be difficult to let the argument go, and each of you may wish to hammer your point into the ground (like endlessly pushing the elevator call button in hopes that the elevator will arrive faster), at some point it is best to agree that an agreement will not be reached. Then you can both walk away shaking your heads at how bullheaded your partner can be, how he lacks even the semblance of common sense, and stupidly but smugly smile at the correctness of your position. While not a complete victory, it provides for each spouse a reasonable amount of peace and a sense of relief that the battle is over.

Of course, the most magical part of this prolonged arguing to prove one's point is that you discover over time that most discussions do not mean much and likely are of the utmost unimportance in the larger scheme of life. You will find, after several years of marriage, that very little is worth fighting about and you may even conclude that life is too short to put a lot of energy into trivial matters.

Say "I agree" as much as possible. And if you can't agree, then just agree to disagree.

Mention how nice your spouse looks

I don't know why, but we tend to be stingy with compliments. They don't take much time and they certainly don't cost any money, but we withhold them.

When was the last time that you really complimented your wife on her looks? Have you noticed a new outfit or haircut? It doesn't take much effort. Mention your husband's new shirt or sports coat. Observe your wife's new hair color and glasses. Especially as we get a few miles on us, a compliment is really appreciated.

We all look pretty good when we are twenty, but as we approach fifty, we face a whole different challenge. We have to work at just maintenance, leave aside improvement. Notice the efforts that she makes to look good, that he makes to take care of himself. Encourage each other to buy some new clothes and try some new styles. You may even want to shop together.

Have an attitude of gratitude

Part of the problem with money is that people want more. Americans love money. We are often quite focused on it. Thanks to fifty years of television, radio, and other mass media pushing merchandise at us, we are convinced that more will make us happier. We are told that the pursuit of material things will make our lives better and more comfortable. We feel we deserve it; after all, we work hard. We should buy it if we really want it. The idea of delayed gratification gets tossed aside as we pursue the American dream, which too often is simply the pursuit of affluence.

There is increasing evidence, however, that the pursuit of affluence has damaging psychological effects and can damage relationships. In a series of case studies dating to 1993, Ryan and Kasser examined the effects of pursuing money and material goods. Focusing excessively on obtaining wealth was found to create a lower sense of well-being and self-esteem. Feeling more insecure and negative about oneself was not tied to how much money a person already had or what age or nationality they were. Everyone who sought affluence as a primary goal had a lower score for happiness.

The researchers found that people who focused on "intrinsic values" or inner goals experienced a higher sense of vitality, fulfillment, and self-actualization.[13] And the irony was that these people were actually more likely to find wealth because they worked on developing their own talents and personal attributes. Wealth becomes a by-product of personal success.

In spite of research to the contrary, many people still believe that more will make them happier. "The avarice of mankind is insatiable," wrote Aristotle twenty-three centuries ago, in describing the human tendency to have a new desire as soon as an old desire is satisfied.[14]

For decades, Lewis Lapham has been asking people how much money they would need to be happy. "No matter what their income," he reports, "a depressing number of Americans believe that if only they had twice as much, they would inherit the estate of happiness promised them in the Declaration of Independence. The man who receives $15,000 a year is sure that he could relieve his sorrow if he had only $30,000 a year; the man with $1 million a year knows that all would be well if he had $2 million a year. . . . Nobody," he concludes, "ever has enough."[15]

Now, I know what you're thinking—$1 million or $2 million would be enough for me. Actually, you might even think that a much lower sum would work just fine. But the research does not support a magic number at which point we suddenly breathe a sigh of relief, stack our gold coins on the closet shelf, and rest assured that our lives and future are financially secure. To the contrary, new affluence seems to bring new worries and anxieties, as we hold ourselves up to yet another yardstick.

A great example from recent times is the wild financial years of the eighties and nineties, when many New York investment bankers earning "only" $600,000 a year felt poor and suffered from depression, anxiety, and loss of confidence. On less than $600,000, they were unable to keep up with their neighbors, colleagues, and friends. As one broker described his lack of success, "I'm nothing. You understand that? Nothing. I earn $250,000 a year, but it's nothing, and I'm nobody."[16]

This is the problem with money and consumption. Each new luxury quickly becomes a necessity and then an even newer luxury must be identified. We keep chasing the things that will make us happy, but happiness is always just out of reach.

The happiest marriages (and people) I see are those who practice gratitude. They don't worry about having more, they are grateful for what they have. They don't compare themselves against others, for they know that there will always be people who have more. They recognize that the most important things in life aren't purchased with money and that money simply cannot solve all of life's essential problems.

You will take a lot of stress out of your marriage if you practice the fine art of gratitude. Take a few minutes every day to reflect on all the good things that are happening to you—your health, your family, your relationships, your friends. Take in the sunshine and enjoy the moment. The happiest people I know actually write down what they are grateful for and review it every day.

Growing up, I had a beloved grandfather who used to take me fishing. He was a firm believer that few people really enjoy the moments in their lives. He thought people miss happiness even when it is right in front of them. Sometimes, while angling for bluegills on Lake Namakagon in northern Wisconsin, my grandpa would look at me and say, "Well, if this isn't nice, what is?"

That's a nice phrase to use in your marriage.

References

1. Judith Wallerstein, Julia Lewis, and Sandra Blakeslee, *The Unexpected Legacy of Divorce* (New York: Hyperion, 2000), p. 295.

2. Arlene Saluter, *Marital Status and Living Arrangements: March 1994*, U.S. Bureau of the Census.

3. Ibid., pp. 20–484.

4. Linda J. Waite and Maggie Gallagher, *The Case for Marriage: Why Married People Are Happier, Healthier and Better Off Financially* (New York: Doubleday, 2001).

5. Ibid., p. 26.

6. John M. Gottman, *The Seven Principles for Making Marriage Work* (New York: Two Rivers Press, 1999).

7. Federal Occupational Health, "Eating Together Pays Off," *Let's Talk*, Spring 2007.

8. Benedict Carey, "Evidence That Little Touches Mean So Much," *New York Times*, February 22, 2010.

9. BBC News, "How Hugs Can Aid Women's Hearts," BBC.co.uk, August 8, 2005.

10. John Gagnon, as reported in "Am I Normal?," *Good Housekeeping* (March 2001), 72-73.

11. "Furry Friends Can Aid Your Health," Discovery Health.

12. Ty Wenger, "Dating 101: Five Things Super-Happy Couples Do Every Day," *Redbook*, May 22, 2009.

13. Richard M. Ryan and Edward L. Deci, "On Happiness and Human Potentials: A Review of Research on Eudaimonic Well-Being," *Annual Review of Psychology* 52 (February 2001).

14. Aristotle, *Politics*, quoted in Goldian VandenBroeck, ed., *Less Is More: The Art of Voluntary Poverty* (Rochester, Vt.: Inner Traditions, 1996), p. 978.

15. Lewis H. Lapham, *Money and Class in America: Notes and Observations on Our Civil Religion* (New York: Weidenfeld & Nicolson, 1988).

16. Brooke Kroeger, "Feeling Poor on $600,000 a Year," *New York Times*, April 26, 1987.